A GLASS HALF FULL?

THE MARSHALL PAPERS

After World War II, Brookings scholars played an instrumental role in helping the United States craft a concept of international order and build a set of supporting institutions, including what became known as the Marshall Plan, in honor of Secretary of State George C. Marshall who spearheaded the effort. Now, a generation later, the Brookings Foreign Policy program has evoked that vital historical juncture by launching The Marshall Papers, a new book series and part of the Order from Chaos project. These short books will provide accessible research on critical international questions designed to stimulate debate about how the United States and others should act to promote an international order that continues to foster peace, prosperity, and justice.

THE MARSHALL PAPERS

A GLASS HALF FULL?

REBALANCE, REASSURANCE, AND RESOLVE IN THE U.S.-CHINA STRATEGIC RELATIONSHIP

MICHAEL E. O'HANLON
AND JAMES STEINBERG

BROOKINGS INSTITUTION PRESS
Washington, D.C.

The Brookings Institution is a private nonprofit organization devoted to research, education, and publication on important issues of domestic and foreign policy. Its principal purpose is to bring the highest quality independent research and analysis to bear on current and emerging policy problems. Interpretations or conclusions in Brookings publications should be understood to be solely those of the authors.

Library of Congress Cataloging-in-Publication data are available.
ISBN 9-780-8157-3110-8 (pbk : alk. paper)
ISBN 9-780-8157-3130-6 (ebook)

9 8 7 6 5 4 3 2 1

Typeset in Minion

Composition by Westchester Publishing Services

Contents

1 A Crossroads in U.S.-China Relations   **1**

2 The Essence of the Conundrum   **11**

3 The Agenda for Strategic Reassurance and Resolve   **17**

4 Defense Planning and Military Modernization   **25**

5 Contingency Planning   **43**

6 Strategic Issues: Space, Cyber, and Nuclear Matters   **57**

7 Communications, Reconnaissance, and
Confidence Building   **77**

8 The Path Ahead   **83**

Notes   **87**

Index   **101**

CHAPTER 1

A Crossroads in U.S.-China Relations

What is the state of the U.S.-China security relationship with President Obama's term in office concluded and with Donald Trump in the White House? Given the centrality of this relationship to the future of the region and indeed the planet, as well as the emphasis that President Obama has appropriately placed upon it, the question bears asking at this milestone in history. The election of Donald Trump also requires reassessing first principles—both because Trump was elected on a platform challenging many longstanding American foreign policy premises in general and because he articulated particular criticisms of U.S.-China relations.

Since Richard Nixon's opening to Beijing in the early 1970s, there has been considerable continuity in U.S. policy toward the Peoples Republic of China (PRC). The pillars of this policy have included support for economic engagement and diplomatic partnership with China, combined with ongoing security commitments to regional allies, a U.S. military presence in Asia, robust trade and investment relations, and involvement with a range of multilateral institutions and partners. This strategy served U.S. interests well for decades—helping pull the PRC away from the Soviet Union and thus accelerating the end of the Cold War while preserving security for Taiwan, Japan, South Korea, and East Asia in general. The peaceful regional environment provided a context for China's leaders to launch a strategy of "reform and opening up," which lifted hundreds of millions of Chinese out of poverty and contributed to regional and global economic growth as transnational supply chains offered consumers lower prices for tradable goods.

As the decades went by, however, this strategy produced other consequences as well. China became the world's top manufacturing nation, and boasted the world's second largest economy, with dramatic consequences for jobs and investment, especially in the manufacturing sectors of developed countries, particularly the United States and Europe. These developments gave it the wherewithal to field the second most expensive military force, featuring a growing range of high-technology weapons that challenged America's military supremacy in the Western Pacific. Workers complained of unfair trade practices while businesses, which had previously seen China as a market of enormous potential, increasingly saw China through the lens of protectionist regulations, intellectual property (IP) theft, and economic cyber espionage. Taken together, these developments led growing numbers of Americans to question whether China's rise was of mutual benefit either on the security front or on the economic front. The tension in U.S.-China relations was exacerbated because the hoped-for political reform, which was expected to follow the economic opening, failed to materialize. On the contrary, under President Xi Jinping, the movement toward a more open and rights-respecting China seems to have reversed course in favor of more central control and assertive nationalism that challenges what most in the United States consider to be universal principles of human rights. These internal changes were mirrored by a more assertive strategy on the international stage, ranging from China's increasing challenges to the status quo in the East China Sea and South China Sea to China's role in global and regional institutions.

The election of Donald Trump thus comes at a time when the value of the long-standing U.S. approach to China was already under stress and skepticism. During the campaign, Mr. Trump sharply criticized not only China's practices but the failure of the United States to respond effectively, as when he said the following on May 1, 2016, promising a new approach if elected: "We're going to turn it around. And we have the cards, don't forget it. We're like the piggy bank that's being robbed. We have the cards. We have a lot of power with China."[1] Following his election, the president-elect not only refused to temper his critique as some analysts expected, but actually raised the stakes to include the security realm by suggesting that the new administration might abandon the long-standing "one China" policy if China failed to address the president-elect's economic concerns.

During his administration, President Obama sought to develop U.S. policy toward China to address some of these troubling trends, while preserving the basic framework of the "one China" policy. In Obama's first term, recognizing many of these dynamics, his administration articulated a policy of pivoting, or rebalancing U.S. relations with the Asia-Pacific region. The rebalance focused not only on security, but also on broader economic and political issues as well. This was generally well received among American strategists and leaders of both parties and among American allies in Asia as well. But Mr. Trump's election challenges that consensus.[2]

The troubles in the U.S.-China relationship do not automatically invalidate the logic of the rebalance. Many problems in the U.S.-China relationship predate the rebalance; indeed, as noted, they helped motivate Mr. Obama to articulate that new paradigm in the first place. Moreover, a strategy must be judged not only by its near-term achievement of objectives but also by the clarity with which it conveys core national interests and the conditions it establishes that may produce success over time. Nonetheless, it is safe to conclude that we have collectively reached a major milestone in the future of the U.S.-China relationship, and a period of fundamental reassessment.

If one dates the formal inauguration of the rebalance policy to Secretary of State Hillary Clinton's *Foreign Policy* article on the subject in October 2011, followed by President Obama's visit to Australia and the broader region in November of 2011,[3] the regional security situation involving China deteriorated in many ways in the following months and years.[4] In April 2012 China moved military forces into position to establish control of the Scarborough Shoal. (In July 2016 the Permanent Court of Arbitration for the UN Convention on the Law of the Sea in The Hague ruled this action to be an infringement of the Philippines' exclusive economic zone.) China also established a new administrative unit to oversee the Paracel and Spratly Islands of the South China Sea.[5] China asserted an air-defense identification zone, without consultation with other countries, in the East China Sea region in 2013. It moved oilrigs into Vietnam's exclusive economic zone in 2014 and 2016. Over the course of 2014–15, China used a massive system of specialized ships to reclaim more than 3,000 acres (some five square miles) of territory throughout the South China Sea, turning seven land features into artificial islands capable of supporting aircraft and ships. President Xi promised, on a trip to Washington in late 2015, not to militarize the artificial islands—but, in fact, the People's Liberation Army (PLA) had already placed some military aircraft, ships, radars, and missiles on a number of them. Xi's recourse was to blame the United States for militarizing the region first, justifying China's actions as a measured response. Throughout this period, China continued to be ambiguous about the meaning of its claim that the so called nine-dash line covered most of the South China Sea in a maritime zone of Chinese sovereignty.

China increased activity near the Senkaku/Diaoyu islands—by coast guard vessels, fishing ships, and even a navy warship—in 2016.[6] This came after several years during which the situation had remained tense but did not seem to be worsening. It is too soon to conclude where things are now likely headed.[7] China had earlier declared an air-defense identification zone in November 2013 in that same general vicinity as well. Meanwhile, although China-Taiwan relations were reasonably stable in this period, the inauguration of President Tsai of the Democratic People's Party in early 2016 brought a new and uncertain phase to the relationship.

Of course, from China's viewpoint, a number of developments look concerning as well. From Beijing's point of view, American freedom of navigation maneuvers using warships in the South China Sea are provocative; ongoing U.S. military reconnaissance activities near China's littorals are overbearing; Japan's uncompromising attitude on the Senkaku/Diaoyu is, for China, another example of Tokyo's inability to handle the history question fairly.

Then there are issues that could break either way, for good or for bad in the U.S.-China relationship. For example, even if Beijing and Washington largely agree on the desirability of a nonnuclear and nonthreatening North Korea, neither has found a successful strategy to achieve that outcome. The November 2016 decision by Beijing and Washington to limit North Korean coal exports may reflect movement to consensus; conversely, it may prove just the latest example of a sanctions policy that either is not well implemented or not successful in changing the calculus of North Korean decisionmakers. If a crisis erupts and then deteriorates into war, United States and China's commitments to their respective allies would pose a risk of directly clashing with each other.

Despite this litany of recent disagreements and fraught issues, the United States and China have, until now, managed to limit the scale of contention. None of these recent disputes has led to the exchange of gunfire or loss of life. Shipping lanes in the South China Sea remain open, as do air transit zones (even through China's air-defense identification zone). Fishing fleets from all countries remain generally unencumbered in their access to almost all of the region's waters. No country has used force to drive any other country off an island or other land formation, with the exception of China's behavior toward the Philippines around the Scarborough Shoal.

Some of the other allegations of supposed Chinese overreach around the world, such as concerns that it is effectively gobbling up large chunks of Africa in a neo-imperialist way, are largely belied by the facts. China accounts for less than 5 percent of total direct foreign investment in Africa, for example, and only for about 15 percent of direct foreign financing of various projects undertaken by Africans themselves.[8] Of course, all that said, we do not really know—and perhaps China's leaders themselves don't know—the nature of China's long-term strategic ambitions.

In this Marshall Paper, which builds on a book we coauthored in 2014, we attempt a net assessment of the U.S.-China security relationship in the context of the rebalance, and measured against the agenda we had earlier proposed. The focus here, as in the book, is squarely on security matters. Other issues are certainly relevant to the U.S.-China relationship, ranging from trade and investment to global climate and energy policy. But we continue to believe that success or failure in managing security issues will be the single most important determinant of long-term peace and prosperity in East Asia.[9] This is not to say that economic disputes are inconsequential; on the contrary, under President Trump they may become an even more contentious arena, given the emphasis he has placed on issues such as currency manipulation, dumping, subsidies, economic cyber espionage, and intellectual property theft. They will certainly affect public attitudes about the long-term intentions of both countries, and thus will influence their willingness to find common ground on difficult security issues. But by themselves they are unlikely to turn rivalry into conflict. Conversely, progress on the security front can help create a more constructive environment for resolving important economic disputes.

Our goal, as the book's title of *Strategic Reassurance and Resolve* suggests, was to recommend ways that Beijing and Washington could manage their relationship, and their competition, through the complementary tools of reassurance and resolve. The starting point for this agenda was similar to the outlook of the Obama administration in the early days of the rebalance; it was articulated anew in the 2015 National Security Strategy of the United States.

The United States welcomes the rise of a stable, peaceful, and prosperous China. We seek to develop a constructive relationship with China that delivers benefits for our two peoples and promotes security and prosperity in Asia and around the world. We seek cooperation on shared regional and global challenges such as climate change, public health, economic growth, and the denuclearization of the Korean Peninsula. While there will be competition, we reject the inevitability of confrontation. At the same time, we will manage competition from a position of strength while insisting that China uphold international rules and norms on issues ranging from maritime security to trade and human rights. We will closely monitor China's military modernization and expanding presence in Asia, while seeking ways to reduce the risk of misunderstanding or miscalculation. On cybersecurity, we will take necessary actions to protect our businesses and defend our networks against cyber-theft of trade secrets for commercial gain whether by private actors or the Chinese government.[10]

The paper's main argument is this: The U.S.-China security relationship is a work in progress, and recent trends are mixed. The glass is half full; but there are developments on both sides that could portend a more dangerous future.

On the worrying side, there is much to address, and improve, in the U.S.-China relationship today. That is particularly true in regard to Chinese maritime and land reclamation activities as well as the broad domain of cyberspace. Beijing's reluctance to pressure Pyongyang to halt its nuclear and missile program is also concerning. The United States has work to do as well—perhaps most of all in finding ways to make clear that its military strategy and operations in the western Pacific are not designed to threaten China's security and that it is willing to address China's legitimate interests on the Korean peninsula in connection with a resolution of the nuclear question.

At the same time, it's important not to lose sight of the positive dimension—particularly given the all too frequent historical pattern of conflict between established and rising powers. Mutual interdependence and common transnational challenges have provided opportunities for cooperation that have, at least thus far, limited the extent of rivalry. From climate change to Ebola to Iran's nuclear program, the United States and China have successfully worked together. Military-to-military dialogue has deepened, even as both sides question the purpose of each other's military operations.

In many ways, the greatest challenge to the relationship is uncertainty about long-term intentions. Pessimists in the United States dismiss the positive dimension as a smoke-screen hiding long-term Chinese hegemonic ambitions—the realization of the China Dream. From the Chinese perspective, U.S. support for China's peaceful rise and partnership on global issues is belied by a military strategy that is seen as designed to contain and threaten China. This mutual suspicion and tendency to emphasize the troubling aspects as the "true" reflection of long-term intentions risks the deepening of a downward security spiral. Part of this book's purpose is to provide a more balanced assessment of the current state of relations and, as we attempted in our earlier book, to propose a series of measures that could help stabilize the relationship, without papering over the real problems that will likely persist between Beijing and Washington.

On the U.S. side, the logic of the rebalance is well suited to advancing the twin goals of reassurance and resolve. It comprises a renewed American focus on the region, including instruments of hard power, yet generally not in a way that should be seen as threatening to Beijing. There is much still to do to translate this broad philosophy into a specific constructive agenda, and to elicit an explicit Chinese commitment to a similar philosophy, but the rebalance provides a solid framework for the future. In some ways President Trump's emphasis on "quid pro quo" relations may prove consistent with the approach we outline in the book—the need for each side to articulate the actions of the other that cause concern, and a willingness to explore mutual accommodation that advances the interests of both.

China is seeking more prominence, prestige, and prerogatives on the world stage, commensurate with its newfound economic and military strength. That is understandable. Yet to avoid dangerous confrontation with the United States and its partners, it can and should seek to expand its influence and clout in ways generally consistent with the international order that has helped it prosper and ascend—even if it wishes some influence over the future course of how that order is refined for the twenty-first century. As for the United States, it is competing with China in many ways, to be sure, and it will have to keep competing. But its approach should not insist on dominance for its own sake, an outcome China is bound to resist. While the reassurance agenda should be pursued much more vigorously, the fact that disputes will persist should not cause either side to throw up its arms in despair over the other's behavior.

CHAPTER 2

The Essence of the Conundrum

Before delving into specifics on recent trends across an array of security subjects, it is important to place the challenge of U.S.-China relations in broad perspective. Beyond the fundamental, structural reality of a rising power pushing up against an established power, there are also specific dimensions to the relationship between the United States of America and People's Republic of China (PRC) that add particular texture, complexity, and potential difficulty to the inherent tensions between a rising and an established power. As we wrote in *Strategic Reassurance and Resolve,* the interaction between these two great powers, China and the United States, is colored by their distinctive histories and strategic cultures, which we characterize as the Middle Kingdom meeting the Shining City on a Hill.

The sense of exceptionalism begins with each country's belief in the virtue of its own form of government. In the United States, this is rooted in the special providence that led to the founding of the American democracy and has sustained it for nearly 250 years. For China, it is the Confucian tradition of the mandate of Heaven, married to the Marxian conviction of the mandate of the Communist Party, that restored the glory of the ancient dynasties while lifting hundreds of millions of Chinese out of poverty.

Even more consequential is how this sense of exceptionalism extends to each country's views about international order and national security. For many Americans, the blessings of liberty are not solely for the benefit of the United States, but should be championed universally. China, too, has a sense of a unique civilization with a privileged role and destiny to be the natural dominant power (at least within East Asia) benevolently providing order to lesser, even tributary, states. As the source of many of East Asia's cultures, languages, religious traditions, and other distinguishing characteristics, it does not lack for confidence. Moreover, unlike Western countries, which are seen as aggressive and imperial, China sees its overall role in the world as more peaceful and restrained, based on Confucian values and a history of waging relatively few wars of aggression or ambition. As such, it feels no particular sense of deference toward the United States or Europe.

More concretely, each country's current strategic outlook is shaped by recent events that color how it seeks to achieve security—the product of powerful and extremely painful lessons that they aim never to repeat. For the United States, the experience of the two World Wars undermined the dominant, relatively isolationist narrative of the eighteenth and nineteenth centuries in favor of a belief that U.S. security could be achieved only through sustained global leadership and engagement. Manifesting resolve and avoiding deterrence failure became the top priorities. Worries about inadvertently contributing to needless wars, or fueling the flames of international conflict in showdowns with other powers, have been seen as less pressing. President Trump's election may foreshadow a more restrained approach, building on President Obama's own skepticism about the scope of U.S. engagement and intervention abroad, including forward-deployed military presence.

For China, a century of humiliation, beginning with the Opium Wars in 1839 and culminating in the Japanese invasion and occupation, instilled a conviction in the PRC's leaders to build China's strength in ways that would never again make China vulnerable to foreign coercion. This sentiment is reflected in Mao's assertion that China "has stood up," and more recently in Xi Jinping's evocation of the China Dream and the past glory of previous great Chinese dynasties.

Thus Chinese and American conceptions of their exceptionalism and their unique role in establishing international order further exacerbate the inherent structural tensions between the powers. Despite the lack of contested borders or territorial claims and the vast distances that separate them, there is an element of rivalry in the relationship. That dynamic need not lead to conflict. The two countries have important shared interests. They are major trading and investment partners with each other. They both have nuclear weapons, adding an extra element of caution to temper expressions of rivalry and complement their mutual dependencies and self-interest in cooperation. Despite their different political systems, and despite America's convictions that democracies are better partners than autocracies, modern China is more open and pluralistic than the China Kissinger and Nixon first approached in the early 1970s in the waning days of the Cultural Revolution. And even at their

TABLE 2-1. *U.S. Troops Based in Foreign Countries*
(as of Feb 2015, except early 2016 for Iraq and Afghanistan)

Country or region	Number of troops
EUROPE	
Belgium	1,216
Germany	38,491
Italy	11,354
Portugal	617
Spain	2,170
Turkey	1,518
United Kingdom	9,124
Other	1,282
Subtotal	65,772
FORMER SOVIET UNION	87
EAST ASIA & PACIFIC	
Japan	49,396
Korea	24,899
Other	1,360
Subtotal	75,655
NORTH AFRICA, NEAR EAST, & SOUTH ASIA	
Bahrain	3,373
Qatar	610
Other	1,080
Subtotal	5,063
SUB-SAHARAN AFRICA	388
WESTERN HEMISPHERE	
Cuba (Guantanamo)	732
Other	889
Subtotal	1,621
Subtotal: all foreign countries, not including war deployments	148,586

Country or region	Number of troops
CONTINGENCY OPERATIONS SUPPORT	
Afghanistan	9,800
Kuwait	11,865
Iraq/Syria	3,500
Other/Unknown	40,266
Subtotal	65,431
Total currently abroad	214,017

Only countries with at least 500 troops are listed individually. These totals do not include U.S. Navy and Marines at sea. Some contingency operation numbers are likely lower in 2016.

Sources: Department of Defense, "DoD Personnel, Workforce Reports & Publications," (www.dmdc.osd.mil/appj/dwp/dwp_reports.jsp). Richard Sisk, "Carter Signals US Plans to Deploy More Troops to Iraq," Military.com, January 25, 2016. David Jolly, "U.S. to Send More Troops to Aid Afghan Forces Pressed by Taliban," *New York Times*, February 8, 2016.

most ambitious moments, Americans rarely promote "regime change" in China.

Despite these ameliorative factors there are risks that the relationship could become more prone to conflict. The U.S.-China economic relationship, while close, is increasingly contentious. Key American allies, especially Japan, have complicated histories and fraught current relationships with China. And of course, disputed islands, waters, and sea beds in the western Pacific maritime regions provide a possible *casus belli* that could, in a worst case, lead to small battles with the possibility of escalation. China might well seek to employ its newfound muscle to impose its will by force. Since the United States is so firmly committed to the liberal international order it has helped build since 1945, including the regional security architecture of East Asia, it will have a strong inclination to resist even modest aggressions, believing much more than small islands or isolated seas are at stake. While it is possible to overstate the parallel to Thucydides' Trap, by which Sparta and Athens went to war due to forces that seemed to some beyond their control, it is clear that the relationship is surely fragile, and the potential stakes are very high.

CHAPTER 3

The Agenda for Strategic Reassurance and Resolve

Given the risk that the U.S.-China relationship could become increasingly prone to conflict in the coming years, our book laid out a number of policy proposals that might promote better U.S.-China relations—or at least avoid unintended and undesired tensions in the relationship that might lead to conflict. They are organized into four broad categories: general defense planning; regional military contingencies; the strategic domains of cyber, space, and nuclear weapons; and confidence-building and collaborative efforts.

These possible policy initiatives tend to emphasize areas where mutual restraint and reassurance can help dispel fears of hostile intent. But, as we emphasized in the book, conflict can emerge not only from a misplaced sense of threat but also from failure to understand when and where each side is determined to defend what it perceives as fundamental interests. For this reason, clear demonstration and communication of resolve is the essential complement to reassurance. For the United States, any weakening of commitment to its allies and other interests in the region could actually undermine the broader goals of regional stability and security. For China, a determined defense of security and what it sees as its territorial integrity will be fundamental to the very survival of the regime.

A strategy of reassurance and resolve differs in important ways from the classic American approach of "engage but hedge." The former approach takes a more discerning perspective toward hedging behavior, recognizing that some types might be counterproductive. Hedging—"preparing for the worst"—can be self-fulfilling by producing, through what Robert Jervis and others called the security dilemma, counterreactions from the other side that result in a dynamic that ultimately leaves both countries worse off. Firmness is needed, but it should be well thought through. For example, robust forward presence is a healthy way of reminding the region about America's commitment to its stability. But certain concepts associated with the Air-Sea Battle Concept, such as greater U.S. capability for early decisive attacks against strategic targets on the Chinese mainland, could produce arms racing and crisis instability.

In our book, we suggest that there are some basic tools available—in particular, the tools of transparency and resilience—to promote reassurance and avoid the dangers of the security dilemma. By directly addressing the uncertainty created by secrecy, transparency can help reduce risks of a security dilemma dynamic. Transparency was a key element that helped stabilize the U.S.-Soviet dynamic during the Cold War. Until now, China has been reluctant, as the weaker country, to adopt transparency as a technique of reassurance, but with its military capability now growing fast, it should reassess. Resilience offers an alternative to premature hedging, by reducing the risk that underestimating the danger will lead to fatal vulnerabilities. Emphasizing resilience can reduce the chances of either side perceiving the need for, or advantage of, preemptive attack during a crisis.

For operational defense planning, we suggested the United States revise the Air-Sea Battle Concept, which appeared to some to emphasize strikes on the Chinese homeland in the early stages of a major crisis or conflict to cripple China's war-fighting capability. We argued that such an approach not only appeared to threaten China's regime survival but, more important, increased the incentive for China itself to develop asymmetric preventive capabilities. We also suggested that the time had come for China to slow the pace of its military budget growth, given that it will soon be approaching half of America's defense spending levels (at a time when the United States has far more global military responsibilities than does China—and many of these American responsibilities in fact benefit the PRC). We also proposed steps for deescalating the arms competition in and around Taiwan. As of late 2016, there are some hopeful signs with regard to aspects of the military budget and modernization subject.

On contingency planning, we proposed emphasizing crisis response approaches that allowed for de-escalation as well as escalation, avoiding the reflexive resort to tit-for-tat responses. We also favored broadening the tool kit to include asymmetric and non-kinetic military options for both sides, especially in tense areas such as the South China Sea where U.S. and Chinese forces are likely to remain in close proximity for many years to come. We also suggested that China curtail some of its more assertive behaviors in that region as a critical opportunity for reassurance. On Korea, our suggestions include ideas for the two sides to develop cooperative plans to handle military aspects of any future contingency sparked by North Korea; even if the PRC and United States find themselves with opposing allies in this theater, there are credible ways for them to cooperate in any actual conflict. On this set of issues, generally speaking, there has been very limited progress and in fact some regression—though it is easy to imagine how things could be much worse as well.

On strategic issues—those involving nuclear weapons, missile defenses, space systems, and cyber issues in particular—we made a number of recommendations. The United States should continue to seek ways to show greater restraint in its offensive nuclear force planning, to the extent that the need to maintain effective nuclear and conventional deterrence against Russia allows. China in turn should provide more transparency about its own nuclear modernization plans. Both sides should seek to sustain restraint in the military uses of space and avoid offensive operations or weaponry in space, recognizing the inherent challenges of such a policy based on the prevalence of dual-use technologies and the limitations of verification. Here, progress since 2014 (or any other benchmark date) has been quite slow, except to some limited degree in the broader nuclear realm.

On cyber issues, we acknowledged the difficulty of providing confidence and reassurance in this domain, but argued that effective Chinese measures to address cyber economic espionage, and more cooperation against malevolent cyber actions by third parties, could help mitigate suspicions to some degree. Here recent actions by China and the resumption of bilateral dialogue have provided some incipient positive results.

Finally, on confidence building and communications, we offered a number of recommendations. One is the kind of understanding reached in 2014 on safe naval operations—a very commendable accomplishment by Beijing and Washington in recent years. That kind of accord should be extended to allied navies, coast guards, and other non-military fleets. It is also desirable that U.S.-China military cooperation deepen on everything from joint maritime operations to humanitarian relief to UN peacekeeping. On this agenda, the progress has been real, if uneven.

To recapitulate our specific recommendations:

Defense Budgets, Weapons Modernization, and Military Doctrine

- For China, level off military budget growth as China's military budget approaches 50 percent of the U.S. level

- For the United States, adapt Air-Sea Battle to Air-Sea Operations, and for China, limit development and deployment of anti-ship ballistic missiles and similar prompt-attack capabilities to reduce the risk of preemption and quick escalation in crisis

- For the United States, restrain modernization and deployment of long-range strike systems, especially precision conventional strike (missiles, bombers, and emerging technologies)

- Mutually show restraint regarding Taiwan: scaling back PRC missile deployments and other military capacities directed at Taiwan to be followed by appropriate adjustments in U.S. arms sales to Taiwan, reflecting the reduced threat

- For the United States, declare that national missile defense systems will not be sized or configured to threaten China's nuclear deterrent

- Mutually provide advance notification of major tests of advanced weapons

  Contingencies

- Dialogue and conduct notional contingency planning for upheaval and instability in North Korea, to include measures for security of North Korea's nuclear systems and infrastructure

- For the United States and South Korea, in post Korea-unification scenarios, underscore willingness to forgo U.S. forces stationed north of the 38th parallel in return for China's commitment to abide by Seoul's decisions on hosting foreign forces and security alliances

- For the United States, develop operational strategies to contain escalation in a Taiwan contingency (no early attacks on PRC homeland or ports, possible pressure on Chinese sea lines of communication if PRC blockades Taiwan), while retaining capacity to support Taiwan in resisting coercion

- For China, commit to exclusively peaceful means toward Taiwan in response to U.S. commitment not to support unilateral Taiwanese declaration of independence

- For the United States, for South China Sea and East China Sea scenarios, develop asymmetrical responses to possible Chinese aggression (including restrictions on Chinese shipping, economic measures, new bases, and enhanced security support to allies)

- For China, help establish and strengthen ASEAN (Association of Southeast Asian Nations) Code of Conduct, including a commitment not to use or threaten force to resolve territorial disputes; restrict operations of armed combatants in disputed waters

- For the United States and China, provide advance notice of military exercises and deployments in the South China Sea and East China Sea

Nuclear/Space/Cyber

- For China, agree to cap deployment of nuclear warheads in conjunction with next U.S.-Russia agreement for 50 percent warhead cuts

- For the United States, as noted, offer greater transparency on missile defenses, and a commitment not to develop a national missile defense capable of neutralizing the Chinese deterrent

- For the United States, cap development and deployments of long-range precision-strike capabilities (missiles, bombers, and new technologies) capable of targeting China's nuclear and C3 capabilities

- For both, ratify the comprehensive nuclear test ban treaty (CTBT), and agree not to develop new warheads (allowing safety and reliability modification of existing warheads)

- On space, agree to ban collisions/explosions that cause debris above minimal altitudes, ban dedicated antisatellite weapons and tests, ban orbiting weapons for use against Earth, and adopt satellite keep-out zones as well as advance launch notices

- On cyber, agree to joint investigation of cyber attacks on civilian targets apparently emanating from each other's territory. For China, adhere to Budapest Convention on Cybercrime. Agree not to target civilian infrastructure

- Create a cyber risk-reduction center, a nuclear risk-reduction center, hotlines, and improved resilience measures

  Communications/Reconnaissance

- Develop open-skies arrangement and mutual observation of exercises

- Use unarmed assets for routine surveillance, and agree on limits for close approach to the other side's surveillance aircraft and vessels

- Create dedicated military-to-military hotline and Incidents at Sea accord (for all vessels)

- Expand joint peace and humanitarian operations

The remainder of this Marshall Paper will now work through this list of proposals, weaving in other issues and developments as appropriate, to take stock of U.S.-China strategic relations at the end of President Obama's term. That is, it will assess this relationship five years into the so called Asia-Pacific rebalance. With all these specific findings in hand, this book then offers a net assessment of how the strategic relationship has evolved as President Obama prepares to leave office, and concludes by suggesting goals for future policy.

CHAPTER 4

Defense Planning and Military Modernization

Begin with defense budgets. What are the main trends here? Some might say that China and the United States, far and away the world's two largest military spenders, are engaged in a dangerous arms race. This is too simplistic.

American military spending has allowed the United States to maintain a global military presence and capability that help undergird a global order that has brought prosperity and peace to the international community since 1945. This reality has helped not only the United States and its allies, but clearly China as well.

U.S. military spending has oscillated over the decades in response to broad international developments and domestic political priorities. Since the Obama administration announced its intention to rebalance U.S. strategy toward East Asia, the United States has stabilized the downward trajectory of its defense budget in the range of $600 billion (including war costs). It has avoided another round of across-the-board and operationally debilitating budget cuts,

FIGURE 4-1. *U.S. National Defense Annual Budget Outlays, FY 1962–2021*

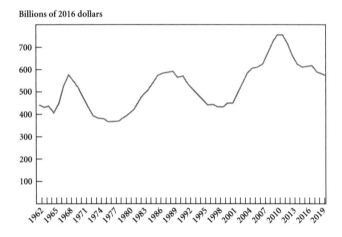

Billions of 2016 dollars

Sources: White House Office of Management and Budget, *Historical Tables: Budget of the U.S. Government, FY2017* (Washington, D.C., February 2016), Table 8.2; U.S. Bureau of Labor Statistics, "CPI Inflation Calculator" (data.bls.gov/cgi-bin/cpicalc.pl).

Figures are based on the president's budget request for 2017. Totals include all war and enacted supplemental funding and include Department of Energy national security spending. Estimates begin in 2016.

known as sequestration, that afflicted the Department of Defense (DOD) and much of the rest of the government in 2013. It has enlarged its Navy by some ten ships over the last several years, returning to a fleet size of 285 ships and is en route to a fleet of about 300 according to current plans.[1]

Higher Chinese military spending, the focus of growing concern to America and its regional allies, has helped that country reestablish its strength. The increase should come as little surprise as it is common for countries experiencing economic growth to devote increasing resources to defense—a response particularly compelling in China's case given its

FIGURE 4-2. *Tonnage Comparison of China and United States Navies*[a]

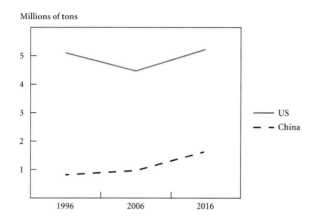

Millions of tons

1996   2006   2016

US
China

Source: International Institute for Strategic Studies, *The Military Balance 2016* (New York: Routledge Press, 2016), pp. 41–42 and 240–43; International Institute for Strategic Studies, *The Military Balance 2006* (New York: Routledge Press, 2006), pp. 32–34 and 266–67; International Institute for Strategic Studies, *The Military Balance 1995–1996* (New York: Routledge Press, 1996), pp. 23–26 and 177–78; NAVSEA Shipbuilding Support Office, "Ship Battle Forces," *Naval Vessel Register* (www.nvr.navy.mil/nvrships/sbf/fleet.htm); James Steinberg and Michael O'Hanlon, *Strategic Reassurance and Resolve: U.S.-China Relations in the Twenty-First Century* (Princeton University Press, 2014).

[a]For China, patrol and coastal combatants are included. Though these ships are not included in the current U.S. Navy, or in the U.S. tonnage here, a large conflict between nations would likely be near territorial waters of China. Any error in weights is less than 10 percent.

historic vulnerability to coercion and invasion by stronger powers. Although the rate of growth in defense spending has likely exceeded the rate of growth of China's GDP (its inflation-adjusted budget has roughly doubled every eight years since 2000), overall defense spending remains at or under about 2 percent of GDP. That is in contrast to the U.S. level that has now stabilized, for the moment at least, at roughly 3 percent of GDP, after having reached or exceeded 4 percent for much of the first dozen years of the century. They both stand in contrast to Cold War defense-spending norms, when superpower military budgets often approached or exceeded 10 percent of GDP. For other historical reference points, consider that the European powers in the late 1930s were spending from 5 to 25 percent of their respective GDPs on their armed forces, or that they were typically spending about 4 percent of GDP on their militaries just before World War I—burdens that quickly grew to 25 percent or more from 1914 through 1918.[2] In today's Middle East, many countries are devoting 5 to 12 percent of GDP on their respective armed forces.

More broadly throughout the Asia-Pacific region, defense burdens are typically modest as a fraction of economic strength—about 2 percent in Australia and Taiwan, 2.5 percent in South Korea (though far greater in North Korea), and perhaps 4 percent in Russia (though with most of that focused on Europe). Defense spending is still only 1 percent of GDP in Japan, despite the expanded military roles adopted under the leadership of Prime Minister Shinzo Abe. These percentages have held roughly steady for years. While there are worrisome signs in certain areas, and while the region's economic growth does mean that resources for military modernization are growing, this is not a set of countries engaged in general arms racing.

That said, relative to other countries in the region, the pace of China's rise has been worrisome. Coupled with its increasing sophistication and focus on power-projection assets, these developments are having an impact on the regional military balance. The purposes of China's buildup have not always been well explained, and the rate of some modernization efforts seems out of synch with the magnitude of any

TABLE 4-1. *Global Distribution of Military Spending, 2015*

MILLIONS OF CURRENT DOLLARS

Country	Defense expenditure	Percentage of global total	Cumulative percentage
United States	597,503	38.3	38
FORMAL U.S. ALLIES			
NATO			
Canada	14,007	0.9	39
France	46,751	3.0	42
Germany	36,686	2.3	45
Italy	21,552	1.4	46
Spain	10,754	0.7	47
Turkey	8,347	0.5	47
United Kingdom	56,244	3.6	51
Rest of NATO[a]	48,451	3.1	54
Total NATO (excluding U.S.)	242,792	15.5	
Total NATO	840,295	53.8	
Rio Pact[b]	52,366	3.4	57
KEY ASIA-PACIFIC ALLIES			
Japan	41,013	2.6	60
South Korea	33,460	2.1	62
Australia	22,764	1.5	63
New Zealand	2,418	0.2	64
Thailand	5,374	0.3	64
Philippines	2,223	0.1	64
Total key Asia-Pacific allies	107,252	6.9	
INFORMAL U.S. ALLIES			
Israel	18,597	1.2	65
Egypt	6,394	0.4	66
Iraq	21,100	1.4	67

(continued)

TABLE 4-1. *(continued)*

Country	Defense expenditure	Percentage of global total	Cumulative percentage
Pakistan	7,456	0.5	68
Gulf Cooperation Council[c, d]	116,297	7.4	75
Jordan	1,603	0.1	75
Morocco	3,298	0.2	75
Mexico	6,051	0.4	76
Taiwan	10,257	0.7	76
Total informal allies	191,053	12.2	
OTHER NATIONS			
Non-NATO Europe	17,499	1.1	77
Other Middle East and North Africa[d, e]	19,754	1.3	78
Other Central and South Asia[d, f]	12,007	0.8	79
Other East Asia and Pacific[g]	21,880	1.4	81
Other Caribbean and Latin America[d, h]	289	0.0	81
Sub-Saharan Africa	21,648	1.4	82
Total Other Nations	93,077	6.0	
MAJOR NEUTRAL NATIONS			
China	145,832	9.3	92
Russia	51,605	3.3	95
India	47,965	3.1	98
Indonesia	7,587	0.5	98
Total major neutral nations	252,989	16.2	

Country	Defense expenditure	Percentage of global total	Cumulative percentage
NEMESES AND ADVERSARIES			
Iran[d*]	15,862	1.0	99
North Korea[i]	5,000	0.3	100
Syria[d*]	2,300	0.1	100
Venezuela	1,205	0.1	100
Cuba[d*]	100	0.0	100
Total nemeses and adversaries	24,467		
TOTAL	1,561,499	100.0	100

Source: International Institute for Strategic Studies, *The Military Balance 2016* (New York: Routledge Press, 2016), pp. 484–90.

a. Albania, Belgium, Bulgaria, Croatia, Czech Republic, Denmark, Estonia, Greece, Hungary, Iceland, Latvia, Lithuania, Luxembourg, Netherlands, Norway, Poland, Portugal, Romania, Slovakia, and Slovenia.

b. Argentina, Bahamas, Bolivia, Brazil, Chile, Colombia, Costa Rica, Dominican Republic, Ecuador, El Salvador, Guatemala, Haiti, Honduras, Nicaragua, Panama, Paraguay, Peru, Trinidad and Tobago, and Uruguay.

c. Bahrain, Kuwait, Oman, Qatar, Saudi Arabia, and the United Arab Emirates.

d. At least some of the data are from 2013 or 2014 because 2015 data were not available.

e. Algeria, Lebanon, Libya, Mauritania, Tunisia, and Yemen.

f. Afghanistan, Bangladesh, Kazakhstan, Kyrgyzstan, Nepal, Sri Lanka, Tajikistan, Turkmenistan, and Uzbekistan.

g. Brunei, Cambodia, Fiji, Laos, Malaysia, Mongolia, Myanmar, Papua New Guinea, Singapore, Timor-Leste, and Vietnam.

h. Antigua and Barbuda, Barbados, Belize, Guyana, Jamaica, and Suriname.

i. North Korea value is an author estimate.

actual threat. There have been numerous impressive results; to take just one category of weaponry, China now has nearly fifty modern submarines, more than twice its number of a decade ago.[3] Its naval capabilities and strategic concepts of operations increasingly push out well beyond littoral waters to the open sea regions of the broader Western Pacific.[4]

FIGURE 4-3. *China's Military Expenditure Estimates from the U.S. Department of Defense*

Billions of 2016 dollars

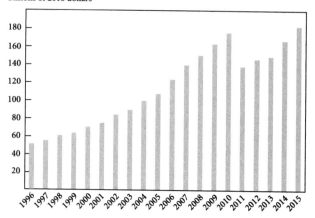

Source: Office of the Secretary of Defense, "Military and Security Developments Involving the People's Republic of China 2010" (Washington, D.C., August 2010), p. 42; "Military and Security Developments Involving the People's Republic of China 2011," (Washington, D.C., August 2011), p. 41 (www.defense.gov/pubs/pdfs/2011_CMPR_Final.pdf); "Military and Security Developments Involving the People's Republic of China 2012," (Washington, D.C., May 2012), p. 6 (www.defense.gov/pubs/pdfs/); "Military and Security Developments Involving the People's Republic of China 2013," (Washington, D.C., June 2013), p. 45 (www.defense.gov/Portals/1/Documents /pubs/2013_China_Report_FINAL.pdf); "Military and Security Developments Involving the People's Republic of China 2014," (Washington, D.C., April 2014), p. 43 (www.defense.gov/Portals/1/Documents/pubs/2014_DoD _China_Report.pdf); "Military and Security Developments Involving the People's Republic of China 2015," (Washington, D.C., April 2015), p. 49 (www .defense.gov/Portals/1/Documents/pubs/2015_China_Military_Power _Report.pdf); "Military and Security Developments Involving the People's Republic of China 2016," (Washington, D.C., April 2016), p. 77 (www.defense .gov/Portals/1/Documents/pubs/2016%20China%20Military%20Power%20 Report.pdf).

China may reach a fleet size similar to the United States by 2020, as retired Admiral Michael McDevitt has estimated. But it will remain far behind, not only in quality but also in combined fleet tonnage, given the large size of many American ships.

Growth in China's military capability seems inevitable, given China's history and the continued advantages in scale and capability of the United States and its allies in the region—with a U.S. defense budget more than three times as large as China's as well as a cumulative inventory of modern weaponry perhaps ten times as valuable as China's. Nonetheless, we argued in our book that as an important measure of reassurance, the time had come for China to slow the pace of buildup. The core argument is based on America's global security responsibilities, which cover at least two major areas of strategic importance and considerable unrest, in contrast to China's exclusively regional focus. Given these differences U.S. defense spending of about twice that of China's was both justifiable and not inherently threatening to China. In fact, given the increasing military competition and tensions with Russia, one could argue for an even larger American edge. Yes, America has more capable allies than China, but it also defends sea lanes that benefit China. In other words, the PRC benefits from American military strength, up to a point at least. Conversely, by sustaining a very high rate of growth, China sows deep seeds of suspicion in the region about its long-term intentions on how it intends to use its growing military capability.

That 1:2 ratio in military budgets need not be a permanent state of affairs, of course. Over time, the relative responsibilities of each country's military could change; over time, the PLA and U.S. military forces could even collaborate on more missions, beyond their current cooperation in the Gulf of Aden counterpiracy operation as well as the occasional humanitarian relief mission today. But for the near future, China could send a significant signal of reassurance to the United States and the region by slowing its rate of spending increases as its budget neared half that of the Pentagon, we argued.

That has not really happened, however. While Chinese GDP growth has slowed of late, it is not yet apparent that this flattening of the growth curve has been translated into the military domain. According to the International Institute for Strategic Studies, China has continued to add the equivalent of some $15 billion a year to recent defense budgets (going from $115 billion in 2013 to $145 billion in 2015, by that particular estimate at least), meaning that military spending has actually been growing faster than GDP in percentage terms.[5] Over the last decade, according to the DOD, China's military budget has been growing steadily at just under 10 percent a year in real, inflation-adjusted terms. The DOD estimated China's annual military resources at $180 billion for 2015, meaning that it could now be approaching $200 billion a year.[6] According to official Chinese reports, indeed, military resources were to increase some 7.6 percent in 2016 relative to the year before.[7]

Nonetheless, it is worth reiterating that despite this fast rate of growth, China's military budget is approaching one-third of the U.S. level—not yet at the 50 percent mark. And military reforms that increase the professionalization of China's defense establishment can also be a benefit by assuring more reliable command and control in a crisis. Among various other efforts, those reforms are also streamlining elements of China's military organization from seven regional commands to five mission-oriented theater commands.[8]

What of the modernization plans of the two sides? China has focused on missiles, increasingly quiet submarines, satellites, and other systems that can contribute to what is often termed an "anti-access/area-denial" capability. This network of sensors and shooters can complicate the ability of the United States to operate safely in the western Pacific region. As such, it is naturally worrisome to Washington and its regional partners. But it is also worth noting that China is not prioritizing other weapons that could be even more foreboding—such as power projection capabilities (for example, a large amphibious fleet that could attack Taiwan) or a superpower-scale offensive nuclear force.[9] And its South China Sea infrastructure, while potentially useful for exercising tactical control and even coercion in that region under day-to-day circumstances, does not represent a major war-fighting capability.

The United States has made major decisions of late on some aspects of its modernization policies. For example, it awarded a contract for the B-3 bomber, since renamed the B-21, with the winning bid from the Northrop Grumman Corporation. With the B-52 bomber force aging, this modernization plan is appropriate. Yet at the same time, it will not be especially large in scale—the intended buy of 100 planes will keep the bomber force at roughly its previous size. Arguments of some that the United States should have emphasized long-range strike systems more comprehensively, through more purchases of bombers, long-range missiles, space weapons, and other capabilities not needing local bases to deliver ordnance in the western Pacific region, have not carried the day.

There is ample room for debate about the right mix of U.S. forces, to be sure. But on balance, decisions to date should be welcomed—from the point of view of promoting both reassurance *and* resolve. Conveying U.S. resolve toward its interests and allies in the region requires continued forward presence—at sea and on the territories of allies. Otherwise, Washington would risk creating the perception that it was no longer willing to pay the costs and run the risks of defending them. Indeed, the United States might need to do more to shore up the resilience and survivability of its forward-deployed capabilities. It could build more hardened communications facilities as well as austere airfields throughout the region to improve the survivability of its forces as well as the networks that link them together, especially if China's behavior becomes more threatening in the future.[10]

In recent years, the United States has also wisely dropped the term Air-Sea Battle. That DOD concept, though not explicitly focused on China, was nonetheless widely understood to have been motivated largely by China's rise. It thus introduced an offensive dimension into U.S.-China strategic relations, with echoes of certain Cold War operational concepts—notably Air-Land Battle, a major NATO initiative involving longer-range precision-strike weapons—directed against the Warsaw Pact in the late 1970s and 1980s. We proposed replacing Air-Sea Battle with a less offense-oriented strategic concept, and a less provocative title—Air-Sea Operations. DOD has moved away from some of the more destabilizing ideas in Air-Sea Battle, and adopted a more anodyne, if awkward, framing: Joint Concept for Access and Maneuver in the Global Commons.

Much more central today is the notion of the Third Offset, a modernization plan driven largely by Deputy Secretary of Defense Robert Work and Vice Chairman of the Joint Chiefs of Staff General Paul Selva with an emphasis on using new and asymmetric means to counter conventional missile threats in particular. It follows what was called the First Off-set in the early decades of the Cold War—America's decision to emphasize nuclear weapons, through its New Look and flexible-response doctrines, as a counter to overwhelmingly large and proximate Soviet armies in Europe. It also follows the Second Offset, a concept from the late 1970s and 1980s that was closely associated with Air-Land Battle. Complementing these doctrinal innovations, former Secretary of Defense Ashton Carter and others have increased the outreach of the DOD to Silicon Valley, setting up a "Defense Innovation Unit/Experimental," or DIUx, with outposts in Silicon Valley and Boston, and more generally prioritizing research and development within the broader defense budget.[11]

The ideas behind the Third Offset are much debated, and it remains to be seen whether this construct will be continued by the next administration. On the positive side, the focus is technology development rather than war-fighting operations, designed to maintain the U.S. technological edge. On other hand, by evoking past "offsets," (and similar technology programs like SDI), which relied on offense-oriented elements designed to neutralize the adversary's capabilities at an early stage of a conflict, there is a danger that their programs will increase insecurity and instability.

Proposals to expand America's offensive missile capabilities that could strike the Chinese homeland received less attention recently. Perhaps this development reflects caution about the approach implicit in early concept papers for Air-Sea Battle that were written in independent think tanks but often with support from within the Pentagon. Some relied on strikes against Chinese missile launchers and other strategic targets in the early stages of war.[12] The notion of using a conventionally armed ballistic missile to conduct a mission known as "prompt global strike," while not entirely abandoned, has been downgraded, along with the cancellation of work into modifying some Trident II submarine-launched ballistic missiles for such purposes. This change is desirable from the perspective of the strategic reassurance and resolve agenda.[13]

China has also continued to develop its ballistic missile capability. Organizationally, China has turned its so called "Second Artillery" Force into a full military service and renamed it the PLA Rocket Force. Technologically, China continues to modernize and expand its medium-range, conventionally armed ballistic missile force, including the "carrier-killer" DF-21D with its maneuvering warhead, as well as the longer-range DF-26 system that could also perhaps hit targets as far away as Guam from launch points in southeastern China. This medium-range ballistic missile force has more than doubled in size, now totaling 200 to 300 missiles, and improved in sophistication over the past five years. This development is of concern to the United States and its allies, though it is a natural development in view of the potential threat that U.S. forward-based air forces and ships pose to the Chinese mainland.

As for the shorter-range missile force, much of which targets Taiwan, the situation is not radically different from a few years ago. Missiles are more accurate but not greater in number.[14] At one level this could be viewed as a sign of restraint by China. At least China is no longer building up its missile forces quantitatively. But since the force was already so big, having grown rapidly in the early years of the 2000s, and since it continues to be improved, it is hard to view the recent plateauing as genuine restraint. In our book, we advocated a substantial reduction in the short-range Chinese missile force—a reduction in threat to Taiwan, which could reduce the need for certain U.S. arms sales to Taiwan.

As for those arms sales, the Obama administration struck a good balance overall. In its first years in office, the administration approved major arms sales packages on systems ranging from helicopters to missile-defense capabilities to combat aircraft. But then its pace of sales slowed, partly due to Taiwan's own stagnating defense budgets (which had averaged well over 3 percent of GDP in the 1990s before falling to about 2 percent in recent times).[15] In Obama's second term, as cross-strait relations stabilized somewhat and the Chinese missile threat across the Taiwan Strait at least stopped growing in size, U.S. arms sales to Taiwan were sustained but modest and consistent with the focus on defensive capabilities, highlighted by a nearly $2 billion deal in late 2015 that emphasized old frigates, amphibious vehicles, support gear, and Stinger shoulder-fired air defense weapons.[16] This may not be a stable equilibrium. Indeed, Obama was criticized for providing inadequate assistance to Taiwan given China's ongoing military buildup. And with changes in leadership both in Taipei and Washington, the future of Taiwan-China relations is again uncertain. But viewed over an eight-year time horizon, the overall policy of U.S. arms sales to Taiwan was roughly consistent with a reassurance and resolve agenda.

Finally, consider U.S. missile defense programs. This subject is addressed shortly in the context of broader strategic issues. But it is not only a nuclear weapons-related matter; it concerns the overall state of the military balance in the western Pacific too, since the same missile defenses that could seek to defend against nuclear-tipped threats would also be charged with addressing conventionally armed missiles.

In terms of official missile defense policy, dating back to the February 2010 Ballistic Missile Defense Review Report, the Department of Defense states the following:

> Both Russia and China have repeatedly expressed concerns that U.S. missile defenses adversely affect their own strategic capabilities and interests. The United States will continue to engage them on this issue to help them better understand the stabilizing benefits of missile defense—particularly China, which claims to have successfully demonstrated its own ground-based midcourse interception on January 11, 2010. As the United States has stated in the past, the homeland missile defense capabilities are focused on regional actors such as Iran and North Korea. While the GMD system would be employed to defend the United States against limited missile launches from any source, it does not have the capacity to cope with large scale Russian or Chinese missile attacks, and is not intended to affect the strategic balance with those countries.[17]

Subsequently, in the same report, the Pentagon states the following:

> Engaging China in discussions of U.S. missile defense plans is also an important part of our international efforts. China is one of the countries most vocal about U.S. ballistic missile defenses and their strategic implications, and its leaders have expressed concern that such defenses might negate China's strategic deterrent. The United States will continue to discuss these matters with China. Maintaining strategic stability in the U.S.-China relationship is as important

to the Administration as maintaining strategic stability with other major powers. At the same time, it is important that China understand that the United States will work to ensure protection of our forces, allies, and partners in East Asia against all regional ballistic missile threats. Consequently, the Administration is committed to substantive and sustained dialogue with China, with the goals of enhancing confidence, improving transparency, and reducing mistrust on strategic security issues.[18]

While this expression of U.S. policy is commendable, especially in light of the inherent limitations of current missile defense technology, it does not fully serve the intended goal of strategic reassurance. To date, the United States has stopped short of an explicit pledge not to undermine China's second-strike retaliatory capability, a commitment Washington made to the USSR during the Cold War, and subsequently to Russia. Moreover, the United States and China have not yet had the kind of operational, military-to-military conversations about U.S. missile defense capabilities and plans that took place between the United States and Russian in discussions surrounding the New Start treaty during the Obama administration. The latter were designed (albeit without the intended effect) to reassure that missile defense deployments in Europe and the United States were configured against potential Iranian and North Korean threats.

Achieving reassurance in this realm is complicated by China's growing regional ballistic missile capability, which requires the United States to develop defensive responses to protect allies and forward deployed forces, but which also might be seen by China as having capability against strategic nuclear missiles. And it is further exacerbated by North

Korea's growing missile capability, which has required the United States and its allies to enhance their missile defenses— including through the deployment of the Terminal High Altitude Area Defense system (THAAD), to which China strenuously objects. We return to this subject in the section on strategic nuclear issues.

Where does this all leave us on the subject of broad military spending and modernization? There is no out-of-control arms race in East Asia, or between the PRC and the United States. Modernization efforts writ large are not overly foreboding either, and there are some elements of restraint in domains such as nuclear weapons, amphibious assault, and other power projection capabilities. There is also revised U.S. thinking on what was known as Air-Sea Battle. But there is also an active, dynamic competition fueled in part by trends in precision-strike missile technologies, and the relationship will have to be carefully assessed and managed going forward, particularly in connection with new types of military competition.

CHAPTER 5

Contingency Planning

There are four main contingencies where the United States and China are at direct risk of military confrontation: the Korean peninsula; Taiwan; the Senkaku/Diaoyu Islands; and the South China Sea. With the exception of the sea lines of communication and international waters of the South China Sea, which the United States considers a vital American interest in their own right, the U.S. role in contingencies in East Asia would likely arise in connection with the defense of a regional friend or ally.

Consider first Korea. Of the three cases, this may be the least likely to involve a direct U.S.-China conflict, but given the stakes for both countries and the scale of troops in the area it could easily become the most consequential.

The situation is more fraught than many realize. Given the many interests—preserving stability, avoiding horizontal nuclear proliferation in the region, discouraging provocative behavior, including nuclear proliferation by Pyongyang, maintaining their respective good ties with South

Korea—cooperation rather than conflict would seem more likely. But this apparent confluence of interests obscures the fact that Beijing and Washington rank the relative importance of those various interests differently, with China emphasizing stability above denuclearization because of geography, while the United States and its allies are more concerned with the nuclear and missile threat and nonproliferation.[1] For this reason, China has only begrudgingly supported and enforced sanctions after each of North Korea's successive nuclear tests, in 2006, 2009, 2013, and twice in 2016. Although in recent months China has taken additional steps to enforce sanctions (in part due to pressure from the United States), there is little evidence that China is prepared to jeopardize the stability of the North Korean regime by tough economic pressure.[2]

These tensions would be exacerbated if a crisis or war erupted on the peninsula. Unlike the United States, whose alliance commitment to South Korea is quite firm, China's alliance with North Korea is less dependable. But even if China chose not to support North Korea under certain circumstances, it might still decide to move forces onto the northern part of the peninsula to manage refugee flows in a contingency, and to prevent the movement of weapons of mass destruction onto Chinese territory or into the hands of groups hostile to China. Depending on the scenario, it might also deploy forces onto the peninsula to establish leverage for discussions over the post-conflict arrangements for the peninsula, including the future of U.S. forces in Korea, and perhaps even to preserve some form of a rump North Korea as a permanent buffer state.[3] North Korea's possession of a nuclear arsenal may also increase the odds that any conflict might stop short of a reunification of the peninsula under Seoul/South-Korean rule.[4]

It was for reasons such as these that we stressed the need for measures to avert a potentially dangerous U.S.-China confrontation in the event of a crisis in Korea. Some involved how to plan for a possible war; even if that war is never fought, the planning itself could produce salutary confidence-building effects. Some involved how to think through post-reunification U.S. force presence on the peninsula. Ultimately it would be the decision of South Korea whether to invite or maintain foreign forces onto its territory in such a situation, but Washington and Seoul could together offer reassurances now that any such American military presence would be modest in scope. It might include limits on the geographic deployment of U.S. forces (perhaps modeled on the understandings reached in connection with German unification within NATO). In the best case, the United States and China would agree on a more effective plan to halt North Korea's nuclear and missile programs— the most effective way to reduce the danger of Sino-U.S. confrontation. Such an agreement might involve some incentives, but also a willingness by China to apply tougher sanctions.

To date, there seems to be little if any progress on this agenda. In fact in conversations with Chinese officials and academics an earlier openness to such a dialogue seems at least for the moment to have abated under China's current leadership.

The potential for a Sino-U.S. clash over Taiwan is a more familiar story. As recently as twenty years ago, tensions over Chinese missile launches in the vicinity of Taiwan led President Clinton to dispatch two U.S. aircraft carriers to the region. Although the United States abrogated its formal security guarantee to Taiwan in connection with the decision to recognize the PRC in the 1970s, the United States has maintained a complex but still ultimately serious commitment to the former's security, reflected in the 1979 Taiwan Relations Act and evidenced in America's actual behavior during the crisis of 1995–96. Although the United States has been careful not to give Taiwan an unconditional guarantee, there is every reason to expect that the United States would not stand idly by in the face of Chinese efforts to force unification with the mainland. This includes the possibility that the United States would resort to force, for example, to defend the island against whatever form of attack mainland China might launch, up to and including a possible invasion, or to provide help in breaking a Chinese blockade.

Today, these possible military missions have become far more complicated, especially against blockade operations or other acts of limited war. China's advanced missile capabilities, quiet submarines, and modern "fourth-generation" aircraft lead the list of technologies that could put U.S. forces at considerable risk in any combat operations near Taiwan, even in the event that the United States with Taiwan could still emerge victorious. Knowing this, in the event of war, Washington could feel early pressures for escalation to protect its own forces as well as Taiwan, especially to neutralize Chinese military assets on the mainland like missile launchers, airfields, and submarine bases. A small conflict could thus rapidly and dangerously escalate. Some steps such as a possible Taiwan-PRC hotline have been proposed that could help stabilize a given situation—if both parties really wanted that.[5] But crises could take on lives of their own, and escalation could result.

Aware of this, we encouraged development of possible asymmetric U.S. responses to Chinese coercion against Taiwan. Military options of the traditional sort would not need to be discarded as a matter of principle. But depending on the nature of the Chinese coercive actions, one could consider either economic responses (in the form of strong, sweeping sanctions) or asymmetric military responses (for example, pressure on the sea lines of communication that China needs to import oil and ship out consumer goods).

It is unclear whether the United States is currently considering these kinds of alternatives. In the section on "Taiwan's Defensive Capabilities" in the annual DOD report to Congress from 2016, no new initiatives for how the United States and Taiwan might collaborate in any new defense concepts are mentioned. America's described role in cross-strait security centers on arms sales and diplomacy.[6] The early 2016 posture statement of Admiral Harry Harris, combatant commander at Pacific Command, states somewhat innocuously, "USPACOM will continue to fulfill U.S. commitments under the Taiwan Relations Act."[7]

Obviously, one would not expect classified war plans to be summarized in public documents. At the same time, deterrence is enhanced by the credibility of the response—and the greater the range of options short of early escalation to attacks on the Chinese mainland, the more likely the United States will in fact respond to coercion. The relative tranquility of cross-strait relations may account for the lack of attention to crisis management options, but with new leadership in Taiwan and the United States—and a more assertive leadership in Beijing that emphasizes defense of Chinese sovereignty—there is a compelling need to rethink the approach.[8] More is surely happening quietly in U.S.-Taiwan security collaboration.[9] But even if more nuanced planning concepts are being developed within private U.S.-Taiwan channels, there is value in promoting greater awareness of the alternatives in the wider strategic and political community and most politicians have not studied or internalized these developments. There is also a critical need to engage not just PACOM and military planners, but the full range of U.S. agencies that can broaden the scope of potential responses—military, economic, and diplomatic—under the aegis of the National Security Council.

In the past several years, growing tensions between Japan and China over the Senkaku/Diaoyu islands have created another potential arena for Sino-U.S. confrontation. Those eight uninhabited, and nearly uninhabitable, specks of land (only one of them larger than a square kilometer) have nonetheless been hugely contentious in Japan-China relations because they conjure up history and reignite old disputes. China lays claim to them based on a historic connection to the Ryukyu Empire and ancient history, not unlike the basis for its claims to much of the South China Sea. China asserts that Japanese control arose from the Treaty of Shimonoseki of 1895 and thus was included in the post-World War II settlement that provided for the return of Chinese territory— including Taiwan—to China. Japan by contrast argues that it acquired the islands as *terra nulla*—unoccupied and unclaimed—prior to the treaty, meaning they were not subject to reversion to China. Following World War II, the United States gained administrative control of the islands and, in 1972, gave administrative control to Japan. This modern history is important because the U.S.-Japan security treaty covers all territory "administered" by Japan—irrespective of whether Japan has sovereignty—thus committing the United States to support Japan in the event of an attack on the islands.[10] That overall history is of course still very poignant for China. Beijing tends to view any and all Japanese land holdings that were established in the late nineteenth and early twentieth centuries as illegitimate and the product of an aggressive tendency in Japanese politics that ultimately gave rise to the Japanese invasion of the Chinese mainland itself.

The issue of the status of the islands lay dormant for many years. At the time of normalization of Sino-Japanese diplomatic relations, the two sides agreed to put the issue aside for later generations to resolve. With the discovery of subsea energy resources and increasing focus on fisheries in the surrounding waters the salience of the territorial claims grew. Though in the mid-2000s the two sides agreed to joint exploration in the East China Sea, tensions have intensified in recent years, with each side blaming the other for stoking conflict. In 2010, a Chinese fishing boat collided with two Japanese Coast Guard vessels near the islands. That led to the arrest of the Chinese boat captain and a prolonged diplomatic row between the two countries that included imposition of Chinese economic sanctions against Japan for a time (specifically, limits on Chinese exports to Japan of rare-earth metals, crucial in some types of manufacturing).[11] Then, in 2012, seeking to avoid what it saw as an even worse outcome if the hard-core nationalist mayor of Tokyo purchased the islands, the Japanese government bought three of the Senkaku/Diaoyu islands from a private Japanese owner. China viewed the action as provocative and stepped up military patrols thereafter, sometimes engaging in brinkmanship around the islands. In addition, it announced the creation of an air defense identification zone (ADIZ) over the East China Sea—an act that purported to require aircraft to notify prior to using that airspace—a claim that was rejected by the United States.

The Obama administration sought to stabilize the situation by making clear (in statements by Secretary Clinton and later in 2014 by President Obama himself) that in Washington's view, Article V of the U.S.-Japan Security

Treaty covered the islands, even though the United States took no position on the ownership of the territory.[12] This act of U.S. resolve was designed to shore up deterrence and discourage aggressive action by China. This decision, and the continued deepening of U.S.-Japan military cooperation under the decision of the Abe administration to allow Japanese Self-Defense Forces to engage in collective self-defense, is consistent with the arguments in our book about the importance of resolve in restraining actions by China that threaten important U.S. interests—in this case our key security partnership in the region. It thus helps promote stability.

For a period of time Sino-Japanese relations stabilized, including meetings by Prime Minister Abe with top Chinese leaders. But in the summer of 2016 China stepped up its activity around the islands, conducting close approaches with aircraft and sea vessels. These included coast guard and fishing ships, well within territorial waters of the islands, according to the Japanese Self-Defense Forces. Indeed, in June of 2016 China sent a warship to the islands' waters for the first time, and on August 6 of that year, some 230 Chinese fishing boats reportedly swarmed around the islands.[13] So the issue has not been solved and is still dangerous. Indeed, partly in response to the situation, Japan is now considering a modest but real increase in its own military capabilities in the broader region.[14]

Moving to the South China Sea, the situation is even more dynamic and complex, and China's recent behavior even more concerning to the United States and several other countries. A prolonged period of enhanced Chinese activity has led to substantial land reclamation on disputed islands, building of installations that support the deployment of military capabilities, expanded fishing in disputed waters accompanied by Chinese government vessels, and most recently the seizure of an unmanned U.S. ocean monitoring submersible in international waters. Despite the growing tensions, however, the scope of the dispute has been reasonably contained, at least until now.[15]

To date, all parties in the region have shown a degree of caution in pushing their respective claims. They are not interrupting the use of shipping lanes; they are not challenging each other's land claims in the South China Sea through violent seizure of territory. There are also numerous communications channels between the United States and China that are being frequently employed—visits by military officials, national security advisors such as Susan Rice, secretaries of state and defense, and presidents themselves, including lengthy discussions that get beyond immediate talking points and seek some degree of understanding and mitigation of conflicts even when solutions are elusive.[16] During Xi Jinping's visit to the United States in September 2015, he announced an agreement to halt further militarization of the islands, although the scope of that pledge and whether it is in fact being honored remain in dispute.

The core of the problem arises from both the expansive scope of China's claim and its growing willingness to use unilateral actions to create a *fait accompli* in support of its claims. Under some versions, China claims virtually the entirety of the South China Sea, including its many small land formations, through its so called nine-dash line. To date China has not sought to restrict transit through these waters, although it has sought to eject fisherman from its claimed waters. It also conducts increasingly active naval, coast guard, and air patrols that have come close to U.S. aircraft and vessels. The importance of these sea-lanes to U.S. economic and military interests is obvious, with a third or more of global trade passing through them. China objects to American military movements in the vicinity but has otherwise not sought to discourage the use of the waters by others. However, China has tried to establish as much control as possible over many of the region's islands, notably the Spratly and Paracel groups, as well as other land formations such as the Scarborough Shoal in the exclusive economic zone of the Philippines.

The July 2016 ruling by the Permanent Court of Arbitration for the UN Convention on the Law of the Sea invalidated China's nine-dash line, if interpreted as a literal claim on the waterways of that region. The Court also determined, without weighing in on the issue of sovereignty, that none of the South China Sea land formations qualified as islands capable of sustaining human life.[17] Thus, whoever might ultimately establish ownership and sovereign rights, they would according to this ruling be granted at most a limited territorial sea, extending out twelve nautical miles from the coastline, and no exclusive economic zone. Mischief Reef and other formations, such as Scarborough Shoal, were determined to be within the Philippines' Exclusive Economic Zone by the Court, meaning that China's construction activities there were ruled unacceptable and illegal.[18]

China refuses to accept the ruling; indeed, it provocatively sent ten ships within a mile of the shoal during the September 2016 G20 meeting in Hangzhou.[19] Even if Beijing were to accept the Court's position, the sovereignty questions would remain undecided, and fraught. Meanwhile over the course of 2014–15 in particular, China added about five square miles of land (roughly the combined acreage of the Senkaku/Diaoyu) to a total of some seven reclaimed islands. It then partially militarized those artificial land formations with missiles, radars, runways, ports, military aircraft, and military or Coast Guard ships. In 2016, Beijing also conducted aerial patrols in the South China Sea, intercepted a U.S. reconnaissance aircraft there, seized a U.S. military ocean monitoring drone in international waters, and sent a senior officer to one of the Spratly Islands.[20]

The United States has conducted several freedom-of-navigation transits through territorial waters of land formations in the South China Sea over the last two years. It has generally done them in a way that acknowledges some country, perhaps China, might someday establish sovereignty. Thus, the United States has transited these zones expeditiously and without conducting training exercises or other military actions—it has exercised innocent passage. Even so, China has objected to these transits because Beijing demands prior notification (which is not required under the Convention on the Law of the Sea). It also does not consider warships eligible for such innocent-passage rights.[21] The American actions have struck a good balance between reassurance and resolve, although Washington could do a better job of explaining the underlying legal rationale behind its actions and conduct them on a routine basis without fanfare, as the United States does with its Freedom of Navigation Operations (FONOP) around the world—including in waters improperly claimed by its own friends and allies. FONOPs show firmness in defense of American interests and allies. Even as China has staked out firmer claims to land formations, it has been essential for the United States not to allow its access to the region to be compromised. It goes almost without saying that the United States could not accept the nine-dash line. However, it could also not accept restrictions on its movements around the small islets or rocks that China claims, and that Beijing has asserted should have territorial seas and also exclusive economic zones associated with them. (As a matter of international law, only islands get all such benefits; rocks get territorial seas but no economic zones; reclaimed islands are accorded nothing.[22]) The United States has remained engaged in the region in other ways, too. Employing some of the seven bases in the Philippines through which the United States now rotates forces (on a total of four different islands), it conducted a form of aerial patrol near the Scarborough Shoal with A-10 aircraft in the spring of 2016.[23]

As noted, China has done its own aerial patrol in the South China Sea, as well, and says that it intends to make them regular.[24] It also maneuvered forces into position to establish control of the Scarborough Shoal at the Philippines' expense in 2012. It has on occasion deployed its forces in dangerous proximity to U.S. naval vessels and aircraft, but has not actually blocked the movement of ships or aircraft in the region. Nor has it declared an air-defense identification zone in the South China Sea to date, as some had anticipated following the declaration of the ADIZ over the East China Sea.[25]

China's military activities, both on the land features and in the surrounding waters, are of real concern although to date they are largely focused on defending China's claims rather than providing a platform for power projection. Chinese assets in the region are now roughly comparable to those of the United States when it has an aircraft carrier battle group in the vicinity. They also have emphasized to some extent the Coast Guard over military assets, or have exploited ambiguities (as with the construction of aircraft shelters that while likely intended for military planes, are not themselves armaments).[26] To be sure, even these limited military moves complicate security planning for the United States and its allies and friends, and represent a downward trend compared with the *status quo ante*, in which the United States had conventional military superiority in the South China Sea except near the Chinese littoral. But to date, China has not sought to establish outright military dominance in the region either, reflecting a form of restraint so far at least. And while it objected strenuously to the ruling in July 2016 by the Permanent Court of Arbitration on South China Sea matters, it showed some restraint in the aftermath of the ruling—still refraining from declaring an air-defense identification zone, calling for negotiations with parties in the region, and sustaining dialogue with the United States.[27]

Thus while the situation remains fraught, a degree of restraint on all sides has prevailed. But it would be wrong to be complacent. Considerable doubts remain about China's long-term intentions. In this arena, China has an important opportunity to provide reassurance to the other claimants and to the international community by agreeing to the ASEAN proposed Code of Conduct governing activities in the South China Sea, to halt reclamation on contested islands, to respect (even if it does not officially accept) the United Nations Convention on the Law of the Sea (UNCLOS) arbitral ruling, and to engage diplomatically with other claimants on issues like joint fishing, energy exploration, and conservation. The United States should support bilateral dialogue between China and the claimants if it is free from coercion, and conduct military activities, including FONOPs in a resolute but low-key manner consistent with principle rather than publicity. The United States should also continue its efforts to build the maritime awareness capacity of its partners in the area.

CHAPTER 6

Strategic Issues: Space, Cyber, and Nuclear Matters

Moving from regional issues to global or strategic ones, how have the United States and China been doing in domains such as nuclear weapons and nuclear doctrine, space, and cyber?

This is a complex set of issues with many different dimensions, only some of those truly overlapping, and thus there is no easy verdict or clear thematic interpretation of how things are going. The relationship has not seen major positive breakthroughs in any of these issue areas, although some progress has been made in dealing with the economic dimension of cyber espionage. Nor has it seen a major effort by the parties to seek out new areas of potential common ground in the way we advocated in 2014. For example, various types of low-risk arms control concepts for the use of space, and certain specific codes of conduct for cyber, have not been seriously explored. The state of U.S.-Russia relations has precluded further cuts in offensive arms by the nuclear superpowers that could have provided an opportunity for China also to show restraint (by making a political commitment not to increase the size of its own force as Moscow and Washington cut theirs, for example). U.S. domestic politics, among other factors, prevented any serious consideration of ratification of the comprehensive nuclear test ban treaty. In addition, there have been significant tensions in certain nuclear-related areas, such as the expected U.S. deployment of a THAAD missile-defense system to South Korea to address the North Korean threat, which China views as a threat to its second-strike nuclear capability, and ongoing disagreements over many cyber matters.

That said, there has also continued to be some degree of restraint by both countries, and the situation seems not to have significantly deteriorated in these domains. The opportunity remains for a future U.S. president and the Chinese government to pursue more substantive areas of cooperation.

On the subject of nuclear weapons, and the related matter of missile defense, there is at least some limited amount of good news. China, for all the growth in its military budget, is not pursuing a superpower-scale nuclear arsenal at this point. It is modernizing its nuclear force with a road-mobile intercontinental ballistic missile (ICBM) and the JIN-class SSBN submarine, but not enlarging it substantially. And it has again formally hewed to a nuclear no-first use policy after having created some ambiguity on that matter in 2014.[1] Unlike the parties to the U.S.-Soviet competition, China has not sought nuclear parity with either the United States or Russia.

In terms of offensive weaponry, the United States continues to field a very large nuclear force, much larger than China's. But it has continued to scale back this force and, at least under President Obama, has indicated a willingness to go

TABLE 6-1. *United States and China Nuclear Forces Comparison, 2016*

United States

Type	Number	Year deployed	Warheads × yield (ktons)	Range (km)	Deployed
ICBMs					
LGM-30G Minuteman III					
Mk-12A	200	1979	1 W78 × 335 (MIRV)	11,300	200
Mk-21/SERV	240	2006	1 W87 × 300	13,000	240
Total	450				440
SLBMs (a)					
UGM-133A Trident II D5	288				
Mk-4		1992	4 W76 × 100 (MIRV)	12,000	68
Mk-4A		2008	4 W76-1 × 100 (MIRV)	12,000	700
Mk-5		1990	4 W88 × 455 (MIRV)	12,000	384
Total	288				1,152

(continued)

TABLE 6-1. (*continued*)

Type	Number	Year deployed	Warheads × yield (ktons)	Range (km)	Deployed
BOMBERS					
B-52H Stratofortress (b)	93/44	1961	ALCM/W80-1 × 5-150	14,080+	200
B-2A Spirit	20/16	1994	B61-7/-11, B83-1	11,100+	100
Total	113				300 (c)
NONSTRATEGIC FORCES					
B61-3,-4 Bombs	n/a	1979	0.3-170	Gravity bomb	180 (d)
Total					180
Total deployed					~2,070 (e)
Reserve					~2,598
TOTAL STOCKPILE					~4,670 (f)

China

Type	Number	Year deployed	Warheads × yield (ktons)	Range (km)	Deployed
LAND-BASED BALLISTIC MISSILES					
DF-4	~10	1980	1 × 3,300	5,500	~10
DF-5A	~10	1981	1 × 4,000-5,000	13,000	~10
DF-5B	~10	2015	3 × 200-300	12,000	~30
DF-15	?	1990	1 × ?	600	?(g)
DF-21	~80	1991	1 × 200-300	2,150	~80
DF-26	?	(2017)	1 × 200-300	4,000	?
DF-31	~8	2006	1 × 200-300?	7,000	~8
DF-31A	~25	2007	1 × 200-300?	11,000	~25
DF-41	n.a.	?	?	?	n.a.
Total	~63				~163(h)

(continued)

TABLE 6-1. (continued)

Type	Number	Year deployed	Warheads × yield (ktons)	Range (km)	Deployed
SUBMARINE-LAUNCHED MISSILES(i)					
JL-1	n.a.	1986	1 × 200-300	1,000	n.a.
JL-2	(48)	(2015)	1 × 200-300?	~7,000	(48)
AIRCRAFT					
H-6(j)	~20	1965	1 × bomb	3,100	~20
Fighters(k)	?	?	1 × bomb	n.a.	?
CRUISE MISSILES(l)					
DH-10	~250	2006	1 × ?	1,500?	?
DH-20?	?	?	1 × ?	?	?
TOTAL (m)					~183 (260)

Source: Hans M. Kristensen and Robert S. Norris, "US Nuclear Forces, 2016," *Bulletin of the Atomic Scientists*, March 2016, p. 64 (www .tandfonline.com/doi/pdf/10.1080/00963402.2016.1145901). Hans M. Kristensen and Robert S. Norris, "Chinese Nuclear Forces, 2016," *Bulletin of the Atomic Scientists*, June 2016, p. 206 (http://dx.doi.org/10.1080/00963402.2016.1194054).

(a) Two additional submarines with 48 missile tubes (total) are normally in overhaul and not available for deployment.

(b) The figures shown for aircraft inventory. Primary mission aircraft include 44 B-52s and 16 B2-As.

(c) The pool of bombs and cruise missiles allows for multiple loading possibilities depending on the mission. The air force has 528 ALCMs, of which 200 are deployed at bases with nuclear-certified bombers; 100 gravity bombs are operationally deployed only with the B-2.

(d) Nearly all of these are deployed in Europe. (Another 320 bombs are in storage in the United States, for a total inventory of 500 nonstrategic bombs.)

(e) The U.S. government does not count spares as operational warheads. They are included in the reserve.

(f) In addition to the warheads in the Defense Department stockpile, an additional 2,300 warheads under custody of the Energy Department await dismantlement.

(g) The CIA concludes China "almost certainly" developed this warhead, but it is unclear if it was fielded.

(h) The missile and warhead inventory may be larger than the number of launchers, some of which can be reused with multiple missiles.

(i) The JL-1 is no longer thought to be operational; JL-2 may be nearly fully operational. Old warheads have likely been retired and new ones created.

(j) Bombers were used for testing in the past, and it is believed some still have a secondary nuclear mission.

(k) A fighter-bomber was used in a nuclear test, but it is unknown whether a tactical bomb capability has been fielded.

(l) These are listed as nuclear-capable by several agencies, but it is unclear whether the finding is from a coordinated intelligence estimate.

(m) The number in parentheses includes the 48 warheads produced for the four existing nuclear-powered ballistic subs, as well as about 30 additional warheads.

further in carrying out reductions, should Russia be so inclined. President Obama sought to promote nuclear safety throughout his presidency, even if progress toward his nuclear zero vision as expressed in his 2009 Prague speech was slow. He showed interest in shoring up regimes like the CTBT even if unable to achieve formal ratification in the Senate.[2]

Still, the United States retains a very large nuclear weapons capability and infrastructure. It encompasses nuclear-armed submarines, land-based missiles, the bomber force, and a number of shorter-range platforms such as tactical-combat aircraft capable of delivering nuclear weapons. It also includes a large Department of Energy (DOE) system responsible for the warheads themselves, not to mention the multibillion-dollar annual cleanup effort to deal with the legacy of the Cold War nuclear buildup. The costs of all of this are expected to rise considerably in the years ahead, with the annual budget of perhaps $35 billion for nuclear forces growing by $10 billion and remaining at that higher level for decades, given the current plan to replace today's triad of nuclear delivery vehicles and make other modernizations at the DOD and DOE (including deployment of interoperable warheads, based on existing technology, with the first to be called the IW-1).[3]

A large, reliable, safe, flexible American nuclear deterrent is surely necessary. President Obama's vision of a world free of nuclear weapons at some point in the foreseeable (if distant) future seems even further away than when he first advocated it. The Global Zero movement that had originally hoped for serious multilateral negotiations on eliminating all nuclear weapons from the planet in the course of the 2020s, with a possible realization of that goal in the 2030s, no longer has much momentum. Russia's ambitious nuclear

modernization program has, at least for the present, under-
cut any serious pressure for substantial U.S. reductions and
President Trump has, at least in rhetoric, vowed to strengthen
the U.S. nuclear arsenal. North Korea's program has also
highlighted the continued salience of nuclear weapons in
the post-Cold War world.[4]

Although the United States is likely to maintain a robust
nuclear capability for the near future, there is room for
Sino-U.S. cooperation to improve strategic stability in the
bilateral relationship. The two countries also have other
common nuclear interests: limiting nuclear proliferation,
preventing accidental nuclear use, and keeping nuclear ma-
terials out of the hands of terrorists. Fresh thinking about
nuclear doctrine and force structure could also contribute
to mutual reassurance in the nuclear realm.[5]

Even though U.S. strategic nuclear forces have declined
several fold since the fall of the Berlin Wall, the United States
and Russia each have more than 1,500 strategic nuclear warheads, many of which are on high alert and quickly usable.
Significant further reductions would be possible and still
leave the United States with survivable forces capable of caus-
ing unimaginable damage to any potential adversary, thus
preserving deterrence.[6]

Technological advances can also contribute to a rethink-
ing of outdated nuclear weapons policy, with benefits for the
U.S.-China strategic relationship as outlined here. Reducing
the salience of nuclear weapons while sustaining deterrence
(including extended deterrence on behalf of U.S. allies) will
contribute to a more stable Asia-Pacific region and reduce
the risk that China will decide to engage in Cold War-style
nuclear arms racing with the United States. The principal issues in contention between the United States and China—such
as the contingencies discussed in this paper and economic

disputes—do not rise to the level of existential threat that characterized the Cold War. This situation makes the plausibility of a nuclear exchange all the more remote.[7] Although there have been a number of productive track II discussions between U.S. and Chinese experts on nuclear issues, any official dialogue, not to mention substantive agreement, has been rare. During the Clinton administration the two sides agreed in principle not to target each other. But that commitment has little substantive impact and there has been little evidence that either side has been willing to discuss operational concepts, such as moving away from nuclear counterforce strategies to reduce incentives for early escalation in a crisis.[8]

Missile defense remains a major and expensive component of American military modernization, amounting to about $9 billion a year in the proposed 2017 budget. There is a strong case for a robust program at this level, given the range of both theater missile threats and the emerging North Korean ICBM capability. China's own growing and increasingly efficient regional missile capability also provides an important impetus for missile defense deployments by the United States and regional partners. Thus to the extent that China is concerned about the impact of these defenses on strategic deterrence, a path is open for China to reassure its neighbors by scaling back its own offensive capability. That said, it is in the American interest to provide China with transparency about the scope and intent of its missile defense programs. Washington should seek to distinguish between those systems that could in theory challenge China's strategic nuclear deterrent and those that cannot.

Throughout the Obama presidency, missile defense budgets remained at real-dollar levels comparable to those of Ronald Reagan's Strategic Defense Initiative, even if the goal of Reagan's SDI to render nuclear weapons "impotent and obsolete" remains out of reach, as it almost surely will continue to be in the future. But missile defense can still have important roles, especially in complicating the attack plans of smaller nuclear weapons powers and also in combating conventionally armed ballistic as well as cruise missiles (ballistic missiles are powered only in their launch and boost phases; cruise missiles are essentially unmanned aircraft that are powered throughout flight).

Consider some scenarios where missile defense could be helpful, even if it were far from airtight or perfect in performance. For example, if North Korea had the ability to deliver nuclear weapons intercontinentally, with warheads capable of surviving the flight and missiles capable of delivering warheads many thousands of miles, it could threaten American cities. That in turn could weaken deterrence in a crisis, if North Korea felt it could persuade Washington to back down from resolute behavior. It could also lead U.S. regional allies like South Korea and Japan to doubt America's commitment to their defense (even if that view was unwarranted), possibly persuading them to pursue their own nuclear weapons and thereby further intensify negative regional security dynamics. But long-range missiles are large, complex, and expensive. So even if North Korea could reach some level of competence on the basic technologies, it probably could not build very many. And the United States with regional allies might be able to preempt some before they could be launched, especially in the context of an active war (when there would be little reason to avoid doing so). As such, the credible ability to shoot down just one, two, or three ballistic missiles in flight might well reduce the expected number of North Korean hits on American soil from one or two to perhaps zero. Threats to South Korea and Japan could also be mitigated, including by deployment of the THAAD missile defense system on the peninsula, reducing fears and providing reassurance for Seoul and Tokyo.[9]

Missile defense is also relevant to a potential, more direct U.S.-China crisis. China is dramatically improving its conventionally armed missile forces near western Pacific waters and thus near Taiwan. In a future crisis scenario, it could threaten airfields such as the Kadena Air Force Base on Okinawa, which would be crucial to any American role in helping defend Taiwan against Chinese attack. It is unrealistic to think that missile defense could make such an airfield impervious to missile strikes. But a combination of hardening of facilities, bolstering of runway-repair capabilities, deployment of versatile platforms that could operate in more austere conditions if necessary (such as vertical/short-takeoff and landing, or VSTOL, aircraft), and missile defense might well sustain a credible and resilient American military capability well into the future. The odds of successful defense are even stronger in Guam, as it is further from the Chinese mainland, meaning that a system like the DF-21D "carrier killer" cannot reach it (though another missile, the DF-26, may be able to).[10]

This is not an argument for trying to win an offense-defense arms race using American missile defense technologies. On balance, the offense will probably have the advantage in this kind of situation, at least until directed-energy defense systems or other types of new technological concepts for missile defense become effective and economical. Such systems are theoretically very appealing, since they do not suffer the same vulnerabilities to saturation attack as traditional missile-based defenses, and do not face the same cost-ratio disadvantages as a system that must use one or more defensive missiles to shoot down a given incoming missile. Although they remain in early stages of development, they could within one to two decades begin to provide considerable capabilities for site defense in particular. As such, research and development budgets for these technologies should remain robust. In the short term, though, a traditional missile defense system can help somewhat. For example, it can complicate any plan by China or any other country to threaten launching a small salvo of missiles to produce coercive effects—because such a limited use of force might not penetrate even an imperfect and modestly sized defense.

Missile defense can also help protect ships in western Pacific waters—which China can now threaten with a variety of cruise and ballistic missiles including the SS-N-22 Sunburn, the SS-N-27 Sizzler, the DF-21D, and eventually the DF-26.[11] Chinese missile inventories are large relative to a given ship's defense capacities. But if China has trouble finding and targeting the ships, or if its missiles' guidance systems and targeting infrastructures can be jammed or otherwise compromised at least some of the time, missile defense may well be able to make a crucial contribution to fleet survival.

The United States seeks more than one missile defense system for these various types of threats and scenarios. They presently include the Patriot PAC-3 short-range air and missile defense system, the THAAD system, the Aegis/Standard Missile naval capabilities, and the long-range national missile defense system oriented around the ground-based interceptor missile and based in California and Alaska. The latter system is focused particularly on the potential North Korean nuclear threat, though it could have utility against limited launches from other locations (even Iran) as well. Current plans envision improving the quality of the forty-four deployed interceptors and their "kill vehicles" that home in on a target and collide with it to destroy it, while also upgrading the radars used to guide the interceptors so as to better distinguish real warheads from fake decoys.[12]

Washington and Seoul are moving toward deployment of a THAAD battery on the Korean peninsula. Such a deployment makes sense in light of the North Korean threat. A THAAD system might typically have forty-eight to seventy-two interceptor missiles with ranges of up to about 200 kilometers, supported by a radar with range up to some 1,000 kilometers.[13] Given its limited range and capacity, it should not concern China—even if the United States expands that deployment in terms of the number of interceptors or radars, as it may be considering in conjunction with South Korea.[14] For almost all possible launch locations, the interceptors could not reach Chinese intercontinental ballistic missiles at any point in their trajectory. Its radar could detect Chinese missiles launched from some locations in northeast China, but not in a measurably different way than they would have been detected by other sensors in any event. Nor should THAAD be construed, or portrayed, by the United States and South Korea as a form of retaliation against Beijing for failing to sanction North Korea adequately in the aftermath of its nuclear and missile tests. American and South Korean officials sometimes seem to suggest that the purpose of the THAAD deployment is in part to send a message to China that there are costs for China in failing to act more effectively against the North Korean nuclear program. But such an argument is counterproductive, since China is unlikely to respond to such a threat, and taking that approach only serves to validate China's contention that THAAD will degrade China's strategic second-strike capability.

These missile defense systems are collectively showing considerable progress and displaying real capability. As of the fall of 2015, for example, according to a Lockheed Martin briefing, thirty-one of thirty-seven Aegis/Standard Missile tests had been successful, as well as fifty-three of sixty-one Patriot tests and eleven of eleven THAAD attempts.[15] All of these are based on so called "hit-to-kill" technology in which an interceptor is steered directly into the path of an incoming missile or warhead; the resulting impact, typically at several kilometers per second relative speed, suffices to destroy the threat.

As far as these technologies have come, however, there remain two main structural limitations with them, and even the planned upgrades to current systems will not be able to alter the situation fundamentally. First, they are vulnerable to decoys that can mimic warheads, especially in the vacuum of outer space where air resistance does not affect flight trajectories. Second, they are expensive. Each defensive shot requires an interceptor typically costing millions of dollars, which is tolerable against a small threat but not cost-effective against an opponent with a large offensive-missile inventory. Thus, the limitations of missile defense systems must be kept just as vividly in planners' minds as their attributes, and ambitions for large-scale deployments vetted carefully against cost.

Partly for reasons of the state of technology, there has been restraint in American missile defense efforts too. The Airborne Laser program, using lasers on modified 747 aircraft to shoot at burning rocket missiles during their boost phases, was seen as technologically unpromising and budgetarily demanding. Thus, it was effectively canceled, reverting back to a long-term and modestly funded research and development effort. The overall budget for missile defense in the United States was reduced, too. As noted, in addressing these and other possible threats and scenarios, today's U.S. missile defense efforts pursue a multifaceted plan with a combined price tag of about $9 billion annually for 2017 (most spent through the Missile Defense Agency, though some spent by the individual military services). That is a large sum of money, to be sure. And the guiding philosophy behind it is still to address threats of different range, speed, and other flight characteristics with a variety of possible technologies that could vary depending on geographic milieu and other situational specifics. But the funds have been scaled back at least modestly—by 10 to 20 percent from earlier, peak levels.[16] For its effects on the strategic nuclear balance of forces between China and the United States, this can be interpreted as a step toward reassurance.

Cyber concerns remain a contentious and potentially destabilizing dimension of U.S.-China relations. In our book we acknowledge the inherent difficulty of providing much reassurance in this domain. Nonetheless there are areas for modest progress beyond the limited success to date in beginning to address economic cyber espionage and intellectual property theft. Specifically, we recommended that China and the United States consider pledges not to target civilian infrastructure of particularly sensitive types, such as electricity grids or nuclear power plants. We also advocated that China adhere to the Budapest convention, which establishes codes of conduct for the use of the Internet and asks states to pledge to investigate violations of these codes occurring on their territory.[17]

It is worth bearing in mind, though, that should a U.S.-China military conflict occur, it is difficult to believe that either side would refrain from certain types of cyberattacks, including quite possibly early preemptive attacks, against some key elements of the other country's military and even civilian infrastructure. For example, not only would each side have a strong incentive to interfere with the other's offensive military operations, it would also be tempting to attempt to disrupt elements of the internal transportation systems of the other to slow down reinforcements in the event of conflict. Both sides are potentially quite capable in the offensive cyber domain—and potentially quite vulnerable to attack, given their ever-growing dependence on information networks. And once attacks begin against a certain part of a country's military cyber infrastructure, it is unclear if those could be limited to strictly nonnuclear systems (it is also unclear if worms or viruses might spread beyond their intended targets).[18] Thus, when one thinks of creating cyber sanctuaries or no-attack zones, it is important to do so with a degree of modesty about just how well any such firewalls could really be established and sustained.

There has been very modest progress measured against this agenda. In 2013, the two countries convened the inaugural meeting of the Cyber Working Group. By 2015, there was a U.S.-China Senior Experts Group on International Security Issues in Cyberspace, with participation by a number of agencies including but not limited to military ones.[19]

In 2015, President Xi promised to have the Chinese refrain from intellectual property theft, and there may have been some progress to date. That said, American analysts seem unsure as to whether China is simply eliminating the more egregious and obvious behavior in this realm, while improving its abilities to carry out a modest set of activities more carefully and secretively. Still, even a partial reduction in this type of behavior is helpful. China has also engaged in a number of dialogues around the world on cyber security and pledged to take action, for example, against terrorists and criminals (even if its definitions of the latter at home sometimes cause democratic countries concern).[20]

Some forms of Chinese cyber theft, if continued, should be viewed less in national security terms and more as economic misbehavior that warrant economic reprisal. For example, the 2013 Blair-Huntsman commission recommended using tariffs to penalize sectors of the Chinese economy that might benefit from such theft. There is considerable logic in this paradigm, as Ashley Tellis and Robert Blackwill have also argued.[21]

The recent intelligence community allegations about Russian hacking in connection with the 2016 U.S. election and the possibility that such activity could include civilian infrastructure, such as financial systems and U.S. power grids, demonstrates how consequential the cyber realm can be for sowing mistrust. Thus while finding opportunities for reassurance is difficult, there is a powerful incentive to explore even modest steps. Similarly, given the dangers, the importance of showing resolve in the face of unacceptable cyber activity is equally clear. In this respect, the sanctions imposed in recent years both on Russia and China for cyber interference are a welcome step. While prudence dictates the avoidance of reflexive tit-for-tat responses, which can be counterproductive, creative measures are necessary to complement the elaboration of shared norms in this domain.

Regarding space, the situation has not changed significantly over the last five years. Both sides are strengthening their reconnaissance and communications capabilities. China for example has been deploying a satellite navigation system of its own, known as BeiDou. The United States has been deploying enhanced GPS satellites as well as new communications and early warning and other reconnaissance systems (for example, SBIRS, Wideband Global Satcom, and others). These have either greater resilience to specific types of jamming and other interference, more redundancy in their numbers and deployments, or both. American space surveillance capabilities have also been improved. The United States is also seeking to rebuild and make more innovative and economical its domestic space launch industrial and supplier base.[22] These efforts comport with the suggested emphasis on resoluteness and resilience that we offered in our book.

Beyond these developments, the United States and China have not made serious efforts to mitigate crisis instability or avoid a space-related arms race. China has probably continued to develop antisatellite capabilities, though it has not tested them in the way it did in 2007 when it brought down a satellite target. The United States has no dedicated antisatellite program of its own. But most U.S. missile defense systems have inherent antisatellite weapons potential as well—and the United States has missile defense systems in abundance. At the same time, space continues to be more and more populated with satellites as well as debris. While events deliberately designed to cause explosions or collisions and thus produce more debris are relatively rare (except at very low altitudes, where the debris will quickly fall back to Earth), the opportunity to harvest low-hanging fruit with an accord that would limit such activities has not been seized.[23]

In conclusion, there have been some notable if subtle and modest signs of restraint on the nuclear competition between China and the United States. The conventional missile/missile defense competition remains robust at the theater level, but the situation is more restrained at the strategic nuclear level. There have been a few steps forward on the cyber front, though that domain of interaction remains quite worrisome on balance. And on space, the risks remain unchanged, but continue to represent a serious danger in a crisis. The net trend in this broad domain of strategic issues is roughly neutral.

CHAPTER 7

Communications, Reconnaissance, and Confidence Building

There is a final basket of security-related issues crucial in the U.S.-China relationship. They can be loosely organized under the heading of confidence-building efforts, transparency activities, and cooperative ventures. They are not all feel-good subjects, however, because the flip side of many of them can lead to distrust, rivalry, or even crisis. For example, reconnaissance activities can promote transparency, but they can also produce tension, distrust, and close and unfriendly encounters between the military assets of the two countries. Thus, this category of subjects is important both for the good they can do the relationship as well as the harm and danger they can create.

In our book we argued for several policy initiatives. We made the case for an Open-Skies reconnaissance regime patterned after the NATO-Warsaw Pact accord of a quarter century earlier. We proposed better military-to-military hotlines, clearer protocols on how militaries should operate when in each other's proximities, and collaborative efforts where possible on exercises, humanitarian relief, counterpiracy, and peacekeeping missions, not only between the two countries but also with other international partners. We also suggested that there are areas where the United States could modify its forward reconnaissance actions to achieve necessary information gathering by means that China might find less off-putting.

In the reconnaissance area, including Open Skies, there has not been notable progress. As China's regional and global interests grow, its own reconnaissance efforts are growing, as evidenced by its apparent interest in a system of underwater sensors in the South China Sea (similar to the U.S. sound surveillance systems, SOSUS, from the Cold War) and expansion of its monitoring operations in Australia and Djibouti (including the construction of what appears to be a naval port in the latter location).

On other matters, however, there has been headway. Key steps include the following:

- China was quite cooperative in the 2014 search for the missing Malaysian Airlines MH370 aircraft. Many Chinese were aboard the plane, providing ample motivation for Beijing, but its cooperative approach was nonetheless noted and appreciated by other regional states such as Australia.[1]

- China has been generally helpful in Afghanistan as well. In recent years, it has initiated a modest security assistance program. The motives may not be purely altruistic of course; China deals with Islamist extremism on its own territory and also has economic ambitions within Afghanistan that depend on a tolerable security environment. But the important point here is that such aid is being offered in a country with ongoing strong security ties to the United States and West in general. China's willingness to collaborate is thus notable and constructive.[2]

- China continues to expand its roles in UN peacekeeping missions. It now deploys about 3,000 personnel to ten missions, up from 2,200 in 2014, constituting the largest number among any of the Permanent Five members of the United Nations. It sent a battalion of 700 troops to South Sudan in 2015, the first time it had deployed such a formation as part of a UN mission. It also continues its counterpiracy cooperation in the Gulf of Aden.[3] Again, this suggests a greater inclination by China to play a constructive role in promoting and upholding the international order.

- China remains wary about humanitarian military interventions of the type sometimes conducted by Western nations. Yet it is not categorical or dogmatic in these views, especially when compared with past patterns of behavior. For example, it abstained from the UN Security Council vote in 2011 authorizing the use of force to protect civilians in Libya, and while it may have been critical of the role of NATO in contributing to Qaddafi's overthrow, it was far less vociferous in its critiques than was Russia.

- Military hotlines are now in use between the two countries. They have been employed at least five times. That is good news, and constitutes progress. It is not clear, however, that they would be quickly turned to during a crisis. Thus, as five scholars writing through the Center for a New American Security advocate, the two sides may wish to try to "stress test" the hotlines by making use of them during a difficult period (if not necessarily an outright crisis) in U.S.-China relations.[4]

■ Military exchanges are thriving between the two countries. An official accounting of all types of military-to-military contacts in 2015 lists twenty-six visits.[5]

■ China again participated in the multinational "RIMPAC" exercise in the summer of 2016, for the second time (the first was in 2014). It sent a relatively large contingent centered on five ships to a multi-week effort that involved search and rescue simulations and other collaborative activities among more than two dozen militaries, including that of the United States.[6]

■ China has been gradually improving its performance on nonproliferation matters. Although its compliance with certain elements of the sanctions on Iran was questioned at times, there is strong evidence to support that, on both investment and energy trade, China showed substantial restraint, in addition to its diplomatic solidarity with other countries involved in the negotiations, thus helping create the conditions that gave rise to the Joint Comprehensive Plan of Action (the Iran nuclear deal).

■ There has been mixed progress in certain specific domains of safety at sea, particularly involving the navies of China and the United States. The Code for Unplanned Encounters at Sea was established in November of 2014 (as was a code on notification of major military exercises). In the following months, according to the former U.S. Navy Chief of Naval Operations Admiral Jonathan Greenert, three of four close approaches were handled professionally and according to the agreed code. The progress needs to be firmed up, and extended to coast guards and to ships of the PLA (as opposed to just the Chinese navy) and to other countries too, but the template is a good one and initial results are encouraging.[7] In 2015, the agreement was extended to air-to-air encounters as well.[8] There are still occasional risky approaches. But according to Admiral Harris, speaking to the *Wall Street Journal* in August of 2016, they are typically caused by "poor airmanship, not some signal from Chinese leadership to do something unsafe in the air."[9] And the recent seizure of the U.S. ocean monitoring submersible is worrisome, though it remains unclear at this writing who on the Chinese side made that decision.

Of course, there remain many areas of concern. As China becomes more active in military arms sales, with cumulative exports from 2009 through 2014 more than twice those of the previous five-year period, some of the clients are countries of concern to the United States, such as Venezuela and Sudan. Its growing blue-water capacity includes deploying submarines and increasing base access in the Indian Ocean in purported support of its counterpiracy efforts. But in practice this access increases China's ability to engage in a broader range of military activities far from its shores, including military reconnaissance.[10] China conducts more exercises with other countries' militaries than before—thirty-one in 2014, in contrast to an earlier average the previous decade of about seven per year.[11] There are potential benefits from China's greater international military engagement, including confidence building in cases such as the joint China-India exercises, but in some cases the exercises seemed designed to send a broader and more worrisome signal, such as Russia-Chinese naval exercises.

Taken together, there are some positive elements of reassurance in China's actions as it expands the scope of its international military engagement. How China uses its growing capacity is a matter of great concern to the United States and others. So China has both the opportunity and the need to provide reassurance about its global intentions if it is to avoid the danger of inducing balancing and hedging responses that could lead to a spiral of arms racing and instability.

CHAPTER 8

The Path Ahead

It has become fairly common, if not yet quite conventional wisdom, to think of the U.S.-China relationship as headed on a downward path. Some in the United States have blamed President Obama for not being firm enough in his dealings with the Chinese; most Americans blame China for what they see as an increasingly assertive security policy, supported by a breakneck military buildup. Many Chinese, by contrast, seem to believe that the Obama "rebalance" is a thinly disguised policy of containment. The continued tensions over the South China Sea and East China Sea, North Korea's nuclear and missile programs (including U.S. disappointment at China's sanctions policy and the U.S. deployment of THAAD), and cyber matters (not to mention issues beyond the immediate security purview, including trade and human rights) give support to pessimists in both countries.

The 2016 U.S. presidential election has introduced a new element of uncertainty into the relationship. President Trump's campaign critique of China, coupled with the decision to speak directly with the President of Taiwan during the transition period, and his willingness to raise questions implicitly about the future of the One China policy could portend an even more competitive dynamic in the coming years.

As the new administration establishes itself in Washington, it is therefore all the more important to make a careful assessment of the current state of the relationship, to identify the risks of growing competitiveness and even rivalry, and to consider what might be done to avoid deterioration. The analysis we offer here suggests that there are both positive and worrisome developments. Despite the very real tensions and risks that have emerged in the bilateral relationship over the last decade, both sides have exercised important elements of restraint out of recognition both of the benefits of cooperation and the dangers of competition. That is why we suggest that the glass is half-full, that conflict is not inevitable. But without careful management and judicious leadership on both sides, the danger of a downward spiral is substantial. Great power rivals do not always go to war, but often they do.

In each of the domains discussed both here and in our book, we offer a number of concrete steps that each side can take to provide reassurance about its intentions, and also to demonstrate what each sees as its vital interests. This two-pronged approach will help avoid unintended conflict and misperception. Alas, there is no guarantee that the two sides will avoid conflict, to the extent that they see their interests fundamentally at odds. Because the stakes are so great, it also is important to clarify and, where possible, adjust our mutual strategies to maximize the potential for cooperation and to reduce the risks of conflict without sacrificing fundamental national interests—including our values.

The potential of both cooperation and conflict has been highlighted throughout this paper. As China grows, its military spending and technological sophistication increase, making China both a more capable partner and a potentially more dangerous adversary. China seeks more security by pushing the U.S. military further from its shores, while the United States is determined to retain its freedom of action and its ability to defend its allies and friends. Both countries have a vital interest in keeping open the sea-lanes that fuel the global economy and their own well-being. China fears the collapse of North Korea—but also fears an excessively confident North Korea that threatens its neighbors and the United States. Both countries depend on space for an extraordinary number of civilian functions, yet each worries that the other will use space to harm its security. A similar observation holds for the cyber domain.

What should be clear from this is that each side will have to deal with the other. China will not acquiesce to unquestioned U.S. primacy and depend on the goodwill of the United States for its security. The United States, for its part, will not abandon the field or its allies to Chinese hegemony in the Asia-Pacific and beyond. A fight to the death would leave no winners. That recognition should give powerful incentive to explore the suggestions we have made here—and to induce leaders and thinkers in both countries to go beyond our work to explore new avenues for managing the Sino-U.S. strategic relationship.

Notes

1. Jeremy Diamond, "Trump: 'We Can't Continue to Allow China to Rape Our Country,'" cnn.com, May 2, 2016 (www.cnn .com/2016/05/01/politics/donald-trump-china-rape).

2. See, for example, Kathleen Hicks and Michael J. Green, "Revving up the Rebalance to Asia," Center for Strategic and International Studies, Washington, D.C., January 26, 2016 (www .csis.org/analysis/revving-rebalance-asia), and Scott W. Harold, "Is the Pivot Doomed? The Resilience of America's Strategic 'Rebalance,'" *The Washington Quarterly* 37, no. 4 (Winter 2015), pp. 85–99. On the antecedents of the rebalance in the Bush administration, see Nina Silove, "The Pivot Before the Pivot: U.S. Strategy to Preserve the Power Balance in Asia," *International Security* 40, no. 4 (Spring 2016), pp. 45–88.

3. See Derek Chollet, *The Long Game: How Obama Defied Washington and Redefined America's Role in the World* (New York: Public Affairs, 2016), p. 54, and Kurt M. Campbell, *The Pivot: The*

Future of American Statecraft in Asia (New York: Twelve, 2016), pp. 10–30.

4. See Aaron L. Friedberg, "The Sources of Chinese Conduct: Explaining Beijing's Assertiveness," *The Washington Quarterly* 37, no. 4 (Winter 2015), pp. 133–50.

5. See Thomas J. Christensen, "Obama and Asia: Confronting the China Challenge," *Foreign Affairs* 94, no. 5 (September/October 2015), p. 32, and James Steinberg and Michael E. O'Hanlon, "China's Air Defense Zone: The Shape of Things to Come?" Reuters, December 16, 2013 (http://blogs.reuters.com/great-debate/2013/12/16/chinas-air-defense-zone-the-shape-of-things-to-come).

6. Mitsuru Obe, "Japan Presses China on Vessels Sailing Near Disputed Islands," *Wall Street Journal,* August 24, 2016 (www.wsj.com/articles/japan-presses-china-on-vessels-sailing-near-disputed-islands-1472039715).

7. Associated Press, "U.S. Army Chief Visits China Amid Missile System Tensions," *New York Times,* August 16, 2016 (www.nytimes.com/aponline/2016/08/16/world/asia/ap-as-china-us.html?ref=world&_r=0).

8. David Dollar, *China's Engagement with Africa: From Natural Resources to Human Resources* (Washington, D.C.: Brookings, 2016), pp. xiii, 34.

9. For a recent discussion of the security agenda within the broader U.S.-China relationship, see Richard Fontaine and Mira Rapp-Hooper, "The China Syndrome," *The National Interest,* no. 143 (May/June 2016), pp. 10–18; see also G. John Ikenberry, "Between the Eagle and the Dragon: America, China, and Middle State Strategies in East Asia," *Political Science Quarterly* 131, no. 1 (Spring 2016), pp. 9–43.

10. President Barack Obama, *National Security Strategy of the United States* (Washington, D.C.: White House, February 2015) (www.whitehouse.gov/sites/default/files/docs/2015_national_security_strategy_2.pdf).

CHAPTER FOUR

1. Department of Defense, "Defense Budget Overview: United States Department of Defense Fiscal Year 2017 Budget Request," Washington, D.C., February 2016, pp. 1–2, A-1 (http://comptroller .defense.gov/Portals/45/Documents/defbudget/fy2017/FY2017 _Budget_Request_Overview_Book.pdf); and Department of Defense, "Overview: United States Department of Defense Fiscal Year 2014 Budget Request," Washington, D.C., April 2013, pp. 1–2, A-1 (http://comptroller.defense.gov/Portals/45/Documents/defbudget /fy2014/FY2014_Budget_Request_Overview_Book.pdf).

2. Paul Kennedy, *The Rise and Fall of the Great Powers: Economic Change and Military Conflict from 1500 to 2000* (New York: Random House, 1987), pp. 262, 332.

3. National Institute for Defense Studies, *NIDS China Security Report 2016: The Expanding Scope of PLA Activities and the PLA Strategy* (Tokyo, 2016), p. 15.

4. Christopher H. Sharman, "China Moves Out: Stepping Stones Toward a New Maritime Strategy," China Strategic Perspective, Institute for National Strategic Studies, National Defense University, Washington, D.C., April 2015.

5. International Institute for Strategic Studies, *The Military Balance 2016* (Oxfordshire, England: Routledge, 2016), p. 486; International Institute for Strategic Studies, *The Military Balance 2014* (Oxfordshire, England: Routledge, 2014), p. 488.

6. Department of Defense, "Military and Security Developments Involving the People's Republic of China 2016, Annual Report to Congress," Washington, D.C., April 2016, p. 77 (www .defense.gov/Portals/1/Documents/pubs/2016%20China%20Military%20Power%20Report.pdf).

7. Chris Buckley and Jane Perlez, "China Military Budget to Rise Less than 8%, Slower than Usual," *New York Times,* March 4, 2016 (www.nytimes.com/2016/03/05/world/asia/china-military -spending.html?emc=eta1).

8. For an assessment, see Phillip C. Saunders and Joel Wuthnow, "China's Goldwater-Nichols?: Assessing PLA Organizational Reforms," *Joint Force Quarterly,* no. 82 (3rd quarter, 2016), pp. 68–75;

see also Jeremy Page, "President Xi Jinping's Most Dangerous Venture Yet: Remaking China's Military," *Wall Street Journal,* April 25, 2016 (www.wsj.com/articles/president-xi-jinpings-most -dangerous-venture-yet-remaking-chinas-military-1461608795).

9. Stephen Biddle and Ivan Oelrich, "Future Warfare in the Western Pacific," *International Security* 41, no. 1 (Summer 2016), pp. 7–48; Christian Le Miere, "The Spectre of an Asian Arms Race," *Survival* 56, no. 1 (February–March 2014), pp. 139–156; Jeffrey W. Hornung and Mike M. Mochizuki, "Japan: Still an Exceptional U.S. Ally," *The Washington Quarterly* 39, no. 1 (Spring 2016), pp. 95–116; and "Seek, But Shall Ye Find?," *The Economist* (August 6, 2016), pp. 62–63.

10. Kimberly Field and Stephan Pikner, "The Role of U.S. Land Forces in the Asia-Pacific," *Joint Forces Quarterly,* no. 74 (3rd quarter, 2014), p. 32.

11. Deputy Secretary of Defense Bob Work, "The Third U.S. Offset Strategy and Its Implications for Partners and Allies," Washington, D.C., January 28, 2015 (www.defense.gov/News /Speeches/Speech-View/Article/606641/the-third-us-offset -strategy-and-its-implications-for-partners-and-allies); see also Shawn Brimley, "While We Can: Arresting the Erosion of America's Military Edge," Policy Brief, Center for a New American Security, Washington, D.C., December 2015.

12. See Jan van Tol with Mark Gunzinger, Andrew Krepinevich, and Jim Thomas, "AirSea Battle: A Point-of-Departure Operational Concept," Center for Strategic and Budgetary Assessments, Washington, D.C., 2010 (http://csbaonline.org/publications/2010 /05/airsea-battle-concept).

13. James M. Action, "Prompt Global Strike: American and Foreign Developments," Testimony before the Strategic Forces Subcommittee of the House Committee on Armed Services, December 8, 2015 (http://carnegieendowment.org/2015/12/08 /prompt-global-strike-american-and-foreign-developments-pub -62212).

14. Department of Defense, "Military and Security Developments Involving the People's Republic of China 2016, Annual

Report to Congress," Washington, D.C., April 2016, pp. 1, 25, 77 (www.defense.gov/Portals/1/Documents/pubs/2016%20 China%20Military%20Power%20Report.pdf); Department of Defense, "Military and Security Developments Involving the People's Republic of China 2012, Annual Report to Congress," Washington, D.C., April 2012, p. 29 (www.defense.gov/Portals/1/Documents /pubs/2012_CMPR_Final.pdf); and Eric Heginbotham and others, *The U.S.-China Military Scorecard: Forces, Geography, and the Evolving Balance of Power 1996–2017* (Santa Monica, Calif.: RAND, 2015), pp. 47–54.

15. Shirley A. Kan, "Taiwan: Major U.S. Arms Sales Since 1990," Congressional Research Service, August 2014, pp. 56–59 (www.fas.org/sgp/crs/weapons/RL30957.pdf).

16. Zachary Cohen, "U.S. Sells $1.83 Billion of Weapons to Taiwan Despite Chinese Objections," CNN, December 16, 2015 (www.cnn.com/2015/12/16/politics/u-s-taiwan-arms-sales).

17. Department of Defense, *Ballistic Missile Defense Review Report* (February 2010), pp. 12–13 (www.defense.gov/Portals/1 /features/defenseReviews/BMDR/BMDR_as_of_26JAN10_0630 _for_web.pdf).

18. Department of Defense, *Ballistic Missile Defense Review Report*, pp. 34–35.

CHAPTER FIVE

1. See for example, Andrew Scobell, "The PLA Role in China's DPRK Policy," in *PLA Influence on China's National Security Policymaking,* edited by Phillip C. Saunders and Andrew Scobell (Stanford University Press, 2015), pp. 198–217.

2. Andrea Berger, "From Paper to Practice: The Significance of New UN Sanctions on North Korea," *Arms Control Today* 46, no. 4 (May 2016), pp. 8–16.

3. Thomas Woodrow, "The PLA and Cross-Border Contingencies in North Korea and Burma," in *The People's Liberation Army and Contingency Planning in China,* edited by Andrew Scobell, Arthur S. Ding, Phillip C. Saunders, and Scott W. Harold (Washington, D.C.: National Defense University Press, 2015), pp. 205–223;

and Gordon G. Chang, "China and the Korean Peninsula: Why the Problems?" *International Journal of Korean Studies* 19, no. 1 (Spring/Summer 2015), pp. 97–125.

4. See Van Jackson, Testimony before the House Committee on Foreign Affairs, Subcommittee on Asia and the Pacific, February 26, 2015 (https://foreignaffairs.house.gov/hearing/subcommittee -hearing-across-the-other-pond-u-s-opportunities-and-challenges -in-the-asia-pacific).

5. Austin Ramzy, "Leaders of China and Taiwan Talk of Peace Across the Strait," *New York Times,* November 7, 2015 (http://nyti .ms/1kAcCfy).

6. Department of Defense, "Military and Security Developments Involving the People's Republic of China," p. 91; see also, on this point, Nien-chung Liao and Dalton Kuen-da Lin, "Rebalancing Taiwan-U.S. Relations," *Survival* 57, no. 6 (December 2015–January 2016), pp. 145–58.

7. Statement of Admiral Harry B. Harris Jr., U.S. Navy, Commander, U.S. Pacific Command, before the Senate Armed Services Committee, on U.S. Pacific Command Posture, February 23, 2016 (http://www.armed-services.senate.gov/imo/media/doc /Harris_02-23-16.pdf).

8. See for example, Bonnie S. Glaser, "The PLA Role in China's Taiwan Policymaking," in *PLA Influence on China's National Security Policymaking,* edited by Saunders and Scobell, pp. 190– 91; and Jeffrey A. Bader, *Obama and China's Rise: An Insider's Account of America's Asia Strategy* (Washington, D.C.: Brookings, 2012), p. 77.

9. Richard C. Bush, *Uncharted Strait: The Future of China-Taiwan Relations* (Brookings, 2013).

10. Ministry of Foreign Affairs, Government of Japan, "Senkaku Islands," Tokyo, April 13, 2016 (www.mofa.go.jp/region/asia -paci/senkaku/qa_1010.html#q11).

11. "Boat Collisions Spark Japan-China Diplomatic Row," *BBC News,* September 8, 2010 (www.bbc.com/news/world-asia-pacific -11225522); and "How Uninhabited Islands Soured China-Japan Ties," *BBC News,* November 10, 2014 (www.bbc.com/news/world -asia-pacific-11341139).

12. The White House, "Joint Press Conference with President Obama and Prime Minister Abe of Japan," Tokyo, Japan, April 24, 2014 (www.whitehouse.gov/the-press-office/2014/04/24/joint-press -conference-president-obama-and-prime-minister-abe-japan).

13. Mitsuru Obe, "Japan Presses China on Vessels Sailing Near Disputed Islands," *Wall Street Journal,* August 24, 2016 (www.wsj.com/articles/japan-presses-china-on-vessels-sailing -near-disputed-islands-1472039715).

14. Motoko Rich, "Japanese Government Urges Another Increase in Military Spending," *New York Times,* August 30, 2016 (http://nyti.ms/2bZ57yJ).

15. For a related view, see Jeffrey Bader, Kenneth Lieberthal, and Michael McDevitt, "Keeping the South China Sea in Perspective," Brookings, August 2014 (www.brookings.edu/~/media /research/files/papers/2014/08/south-china-sea-perspective -bader-lieberthal-mcdevitt/south-china-sea-perspective-bader -lieberthal-mcdevitt.pdf).

16. Comments of Stapleton Roy at the Brookings Institution, Washington, D.C., July 26, 2016 (www.brookings.edu/events/2016 /07/26-us-china-russia-relations); and David Ignatius, "In Kissinger's Footsteps, Susan Rice Steers Smooth U.S.-China Relations," *Washington Post,* September 1, 2016 (www.washingtonpost .com/opinions/susan-rice-embraces-kissingers-approach-to -china/2016/09/01/7d440a5c-706b-11e6-9705-23e51a2f424d _story.html?utm_term=.f6ea67b2c7bd).

17. "Award in the Matter of the South China Sea Arbitration on PCA Case 2013-19," Permanent Court of Arbitration, the Hague, the Netherlands, July 12, 2016, pp. 473–75 (https://pca-cpa .org/wp-content/uploads/sites/175/2016/07/PH-CN-20160712 -Award.pdf).

18. Presentation of Lynn Kuok at the Center for a New American Security, Washington, D.C., August 17, 2016.

19. Jane Perlez, "New Chinese Vessels Seen Near Disputed Reef in South China Sea," *New York Times,* September 5, 2016 (http:// nyti.ms/2clHFsy).

20. Michael Forsythe, "China Begins Air Patrols over Disputed Area of the South China Sea," *New York Times,* July 18, 2016

(http://nyti.ms/2abzwK7); Gabriel Dominguez, "Chinese J-11s Intercept US Recon Aircraft over South China Sea," *Jane's Defence Weekly* (May 25, 2016), p. 4; and Chris Buckley, "Chinese General Visits Disputed Spratly Islands in South China Sea," *New York Times,* April 18, 2016 (http://nyti.ms/1quj8Y5).

21. Three were conducted from the fall of 2015 through July of 2016, to be precise. Sam LaGrone, "United States Destroyer Passes Near Chinese Artificial Island in South China Sea Freedom of Navigation Operation," *U.S. Naval Institute News,* May 10, 2016 (https://news.usni.org/2016/05/10/u-s-destroyer-passes-near -chinese-artificial-island-in-south-china-sea-freedom-of -navigation-operation).

22. Christopher Mirasota, "What Makes an Island? Land Reclamation and the South China Sea Arbitration," Center for Strategic and International Studies, July 15, 2015 (https://amti.csis.org /what-makes-an-island-land-reclamation-and-the-south-china -sea-arbitration).

23. Dan Lamothe, "Why the Pugnacious A-10 is Flying Maritime Patrols over the South China Sea," *Washington Post,* April 27, 2016 (www.washingtonpost.com/news/checkpoint/wp/2016/04 /27/why-the-pugnacious-a-10-is-flying-maritime-patrols-over -the-south-china-sea); and Patrick M. Cronin, "Sustaining the Rebalance in Southeast Asia: Challenges and Opportunities Facing the Next Administration," *Papers for the Next President,* Center for a New American Security, Washington, D.C., May 2016, p. 12.

24. Richard D. Fisher, Jr., "China to Conduct 'Regular Combat Air Patrols' in SCS," *Jane's Defence Weekly* (July 27, 2016), p. 8.

25. Jeffrey A. Bader, "A Framework for U.S. Policy toward China," Asia Working Group Paper No. 3, Brookings, March 2016, p. 3; and Cris Larano and Jeremy Page, "Beijing Flies Bombers over Disputed South China Sea," *Wall Street Journal,* August 7, 2016 (www.wsj.com/articles/philippines-fidel-ramos-leaves-for -china-monday-for-south-china-sea-talks-1470565429).

26. Alexander Chieh-cheng Huang, "The PLA and Near Seas Maritime Sovereignty Disputes," in *The People's Liberation Army*

and Contingency Planning in China, edited by Andrew Scobell, Arthur S. Ding, Phillip C. Saunders, and Scott W. Harold (Washington, D.C.: National Defense University, 2015), pp. 290–95; and David E. Sanger and Rick Gladstone, "New Photos Cast Doubt on China's Vow Not to Militarize Disputed Islands," *New York Times,* August 8, 2016 (http:/nyti.ms/2b22bAS).

27. See David Ignatius, "Is a Bruised China Taking a Timeout?" *Washington Post,* July 27, 2016, p. A21.

CHAPTER SIX

1. Fiona S. Cunningham and M. Taylor Fravel, "Assuring Assured Retaliation: China's Nuclear Posture and U.S.-China Strategic Stability," *International Security* 40, no. 2 (Fall 2015), pp. 7–50; Office of the Secretary of Defense, *Military and Security Developments Involving the People's Republic of China 2016: Annual Report to Congress* (Washington, D.C.: Department of Defense, April 2016), pp. 3–4, 25, 38 (www.defense.gov/Portals/1 /Documents/pubs/2016%20China%20Military%20Power%20Report.pdf).

2. Josh Rogin, "Obama Plans Major Nuclear Policy Changes in His Final Months," *Washington Post,* July 10, 2016 (www.washington post.com/opinions/global-opinions/obama-plans-major-nuclear -policy-changes-in-his-final-months/2016/07/10/fef3d5ca-4521 -11e6-88d0-6adee48be8bc_story.html?utm_term=.02682e4e8da7).

3. Congressional Budget Office, *Projected Costs of U.S. Nuclear Forces, 2015 to 2024* (Washington, D.C., 2015) (www.cbo.gov /publication/49870).

4. See Michael O'Hanlon, *A Skeptic's Case for Nuclear Disarmament* (Brookings, 2010).

5. See Sean M. Maloney, "Remembering Soviet Nuclear Risks," *Survival* 57, no. 4 (August–September 2014); Gregory D. Koblentz, "Command and Combust: America's Secret History of Atomic Accidents," *Foreign Affairs* 93, no. 1 (January/February 2014), pp. 167–72; and Lawrence J. Cavaiola, David C. Gompert, and Martin Libicki, "Cyber House Rules: On War, Retaliation and Escalation," *Survival* 57, no. 1 (February–March 2015), pp. 86–87.

6. On this kind of idea, see for example Stephen M. Younger, *The Bomb: A New History* (New York: Ecco Books, 2010); and Wallace R. Turnbull III, "Time to Come in from the Cold (War)," *Joint Forces Quarterly,* no. 79 (2015), pp. 38–45.

7. For a similar view see David C. Gompert, Astrid Cevallos, and Cristina L. Garafola, *War with China: Thinking through the Unthinkable* (Santa Monica, Calif: RAND, 2016) (www.rand.org /pubs/research_reports/RR1140.html).

8. Charles L. Glaser and Steve Fetter, "Should the United States Reject MAD? Damage Limitation and U.S. Nuclear Strategy toward China," *International Security* 41, no. 1 (Summer 2016), pp. 49–98.

9. On this issue and the broader question of how to avoid decoupling, see David Santoro and John K. Warden, "Assuring Japan and South Korea in the Second Nuclear Age," *Washington Quarterly* 38, no. 1 (Spring 2015), pp. 147–65. There are downsides to some of the offensive elements of the Santoro/Warden proposal, in my judgment—but that is all the more reason why the defensive elements deserve emphasis and support.

10. On Guam, see Andrew S. Erickson and Justin D. Mikolay, "Guam and American Security in the Pacific," in *Rebalancing U.S. Forces: Basing and Forward Presence in the Asia-Pacific,* edited by Carnes Lord and Andrew S. Erickson (Annapolis, Md.: Naval Institute Press, 2014), pp. 15–35.

11. Kelley Sayler, "Red Alert: The Growing Threat to U.S. Aircraft Carriers," Center for a New American Security, Washington, D.C., February 2016 (www.cnas.org/sites/default/files/publications -pdf/CNASReport-CarrierThreat-160217.pdf).

12. Vice Admiral James Syring, Missile Defense Agency, "Ballistic Missile Defense System Update," Center for Strategic and International Studies, Washington, D.C., January 19, 2016 (www.csis.org/event/ballistic-missile-defense-system-update); General Paul Selva, Vice Chairman of the Joint Chiefs of Staff, "Trends in Military Technology and the Future Force," Brookings, January 21, 2016 (www.brookings.edu/~/media/events/2016 /01/21-militarytechnology/20160121_selva_military_tech _transcript.pdf).

13. "Terminal High-Altitude Area Defence, United States of America," Army-Technology.com, 2016 (www.army-technology .com/projects/thaad).

14. Julian Ryall, "U.S. Mulling Deployment of More THAAD Units to South Korea," *Jane's Defence Weekly* (July 27, 2016), p. 16.

15. Lockheed Martin, "Briefing: Integrated Air and Missile Defense and Changing Global Security Needs," Arlington, Va., October 29, 2015.

16. Missile Defense Agency, "Historical Funding Chart," Department of Defense, Washington, D.C., 2016 (www.mda.mil /global/documents/pdf/FY16_histfunds.pdf).

17. Andrew Futter, "The Dangers of Using Cyberattacks to Counter Nuclear Threats," *Arms Control Today* 46, no. 6 (July/August 2016), pp. 8–14.

18. David C. Gompert and Martin Libicki, "Waging Cyber War the American Way," *Survival* 57, no. 4 (August–September 2015), pp. 7–28; Nigel Inkster, *China's Cyber Power* (London: International Institute for Strategic Studies, 2016), pp. 97–103.

19. Wu Xinbo, "Agenda for a New Great Power Relationship," *Washington Quarterly* 37, no. 1 (Spring 2014), p. 75; and Department of Defense, *Military and Security Developments Involving the People's Republic of China, 2016,* p. 37.

20. Department of Defense, "Military and Security Developments Involving the People's Republic of China 2016, Annual Report to Congress," Washington, D.C., April 2016, p. 37 (www .defense.gov/Portals/1/Documents/pubs/2016%20China%20Military%20Power%20Report.pdf).

21. Robert D. Blackwill and Ashley J. Tellis, *Revising U.S. Grand Strategy toward China* (New York: Council on Foreign Relations, 2015), p. 27.

22. Office of the Under Secretary of Defense for Financial Management, "Defense Budget Overview: United States Department of Defense Fiscal Year 2017 Budget Request," Department of Defense, Washington, D.C., February 2016, p. 5–3 (http:// comptroller.defense.gov/Portals/45/Documents/defbudget /fy2017/FY2017_Budget_Request_Overview_Book.pdf).

23. James R. Clapper, Director of National Intelligence, "Worldwide Threat Assessment of the U.S. Intelligence Community," Senate Armed Services Committee, February 9, 2016, p. 10 (www.dni .gov/files/documents/SASC_Unclassified_2016_ATA_SFR _FINAL.pdf); Heginbotham and others, *The U.S.-China Military Scorecard,* pp. 250–56; National Institute for Defense Studies, *East Asian Strategic Review* (Tokyo: Japan Times, 2016), pp. 15–26; and Office of the Secretary of Defense, *Military and Security Developments Involving the People's Republic of China, 2016,* pp. 36–37.

CHAPTER SEVEN

1. Department of Defense, Government of Australia, "2016 Defence White Paper," Canberra, Australia, 2016, p. 133 (defence .gov.au/whitepaper).

2. Jessica Donati and Ehsanullah Amiri, "China Offers Afghanistan Army Expanded Military Aid," *Wall Street Journal,* March 9, 2016 (www.wsj.com/articles/china-offers-afghanistan -army-expanded-military-aid-1457517153).

3. Department of Defense, *Military and Security Developments Involving the People's Republic of China, 2016,* pp. 21–22.

4. Ely Ratner and others, *More Willing and Able: Charting China's International Security Activism* (Washington, D.C.: Center for a New American Security, 2015), p. 22.

5. Department of Defense, *Military and Security Developments Involving the People's Republic of China, 2016,* pp. 103–04.

6. Ankit Panda, "With 5 Ships and 1,200 Personnel, China Expands RIMPAC 2016 Naval Delegation," *The Diplomat,* June 18, 2016 (http://thediplomat.com/2016/06/with-5-ships-and-1200 -personnel-china-expands-rimpac-2016-naval-delegation).

7. Vago Muradian, "Interview: U.S. Navy's Admiral Jon Greenert," *Defense News* (August 31, 2015) (http://defnews.ly/1EvSqEY).

8. Department of Defense, *Military and Security Developments Involving the People's Republic of China, 2016,* pp. 124–32.

9. David Feith, "A Pacific Admiral Takes China's Measure," *Wall Street Journal,* August 7, 2016 (www.wsj.com/articles/a-pacific -admiral-takes-chinas-measure-1470436129).

10. *Military and Security Developments Involving the People's Republic of China, 2016,* p. 22; and Ratner and others, *More Willing and Able,* p. 47.

11. Oriana Skylar Mastro, "The Vulnerability of Rising Powers: The Logic Behind China's Low Military Transparency," *Asian Security* 12, no. 2 (May–August 2016), p. 72.

Index

Abe, Shinzo, 28, 50
Aegis/Standard Missile naval
  capabilities, 69, 71
Afghanistan, Chinese cooperation
  on security in, 78
Africa, Chinese investments
  in, 6
Airborne Laser program, 71
Air-defense identification zones, 5, 6,
  49, 54
Air-Land Battle Concept, 36, 37
Air-Sea Battle Concept, 18, 19, 21, 36,
  37, 42
Anti-access/area-denial capabilities,
  35
Anti-satellite weapons, 23, 75
Anti-ship ballistic missiles, 21,
  69
Arms competition, 19, 42. *See also*
  Missile defense
Arms sales, 39, 58, 81
ASEAN (Association of Southeast
  Asian Nations) Code of Conduct,
  22–23, 55
Australia: defense spending in, 28;
  reconnaissance and surveillance
  in, 78

B-21 bombers, 35
B-52 bombers, 35
Ballistic Missile Defense Review
  Report (2010), 40
Ballistic missiles, 38, 41, 58, 66.
  See also Missile defense
BeiDou satellite system, 74
Blackwill, Robert, 74
Blair-Huntsman commission (2013),
  74
Budapest Convention on Cybercrime,
  24, 72

Carter, Ashton, 37
Center for a New American Security,
  79
China: arms sales by, 81; belief in
  virtue of government in, 11–12;
  confidence building measures,
  20–21, 24, 77–82; contingency
  planning, 43–55; defense budgets in,
  19, 21, 25–34, 71–72, 85; strategic
  issues, 12–13, 57–76; views on
  international order and national
  security, 12. *See also* Chinese
  military; U.S.-China relations
China Dream, 13

Chinese military: air-defense identification zones, 5, 6; defense spending for, 21; growth of, 2; modernization of, 35–42, 46; naval forces, 31, 33, 58, 80–81; People's Liberation Army, 5, 38, 81; retaliatory capabilities, 41, 58; strategic issues, 57–76
Climate change, 9
Clinton, Bill, 45, 66
Clinton, Hillary, 4, 49
Code for Unplanned Encounters at Sea, 80
Cold War, 2, 18, 41, 64, 66
Communications. *See* Confidence building and communications
Communist Party, 12
Comprehensive Nuclear Test Ban Treaty (CTBT), 23, 64
Confidence building and communications, 20–21, 24, 77–82
Contingency planning, 43–55; for East China Sea, 22, 48–50; for North Korea, 22, 43–45; for South China Sea, 22, 50–55; strategic reassurance and resolve agenda for, 19, 22–23; for Taiwan, 22, 45–48
Counterpiracy operations, 34, 79
CTBT (Comprehensive Nuclear Test Ban Treaty), 23, 64
Currency manipulation, 7
Cyber issues: Budapest Convention on Cybercrime, 24, 72; cyber risk-reduction center, 24; economic espionage, 2, 7, 20, 57, 72–75; strategic issues, 72–75, 76; strategic reassurance and resolve agenda for, 20, 23
Cyber Working Group, 73

Defense Innovation Unit/ Experimental (DIUx), 37
Defense planning, 25–42; defense budgets, 19, 21, 25–34, 71–72, 85; military modernization, 21, 35–42, 46; strategic reassurance and resolve agenda for, 19, 21–22
Department of Defense (DOD, U.S.): and Air-Sea Battle concept, 36; on China's military budget, 34; and defense budgets, 26; and Defense Innovation Unit/Experimental

(DIUx), 37; on missile defense, 40–41; and nuclear arsenal, 64; on Taiwan's defense capabilities, 47
Department of Energy (DOE, U.S.), 64
Diplomatic partnership, 1–2
DIUx (Defense Innovation Unit/ Experimental), 37

East China Sea: contingency planning for, 22, 48–50; military exercises and deployments in, 23; territorial disputes in, 3, 4, 83
Economic engagement, 1–2, 7, 15
Energy Department. *See* Department of Energy
Exceptionalism, 11–12, 13
Exclusive economic zones, 4, 52, 53–54

First Offset plan, 37
Flexible-response doctrine, 37
Foreign direct investment, 6
Freedom of Navigation Operations (FONOP), 53, 55

Global Zero movement, 64
GPS satellites, 74–75
Greenert, Jonathan, 80
Guam, U.S. military presence in, 68
Gulf of Aden, 34, 79

Harris, Harry, 47, 81
Hedging behavior, 18
"Hit-to-kill" technology, 71
Humanitarian relief, 21, 24, 79
Human rights, 3

ICBMs (Intercontinental ballistic missiles), 58, 66
Incidents at Sea accord, 24
India, joint military exercises with China, 81
Intellectual property, 2, 7, 73
International Institute for Strategic Studies, 34
International order, 12, 13, 16
Investment relations. *See* Trade and investment relations
Iran, nuclear program in, 9, 80
Islamist extremism, 78
Isolationism, 12

Japan: China's relations with, 15;
defense spending in, 28; military
cooperation with U.S., 50; missile
defense for, 67–68; security
commitments to, 2; and Senkaku/
Diaoyu Islands dispute, 5, 48–50;
U.S. military presence in, 68;
U.S.-Japan Security Treaty, 49–50
Jervis, Robert, 18
JIN-class submarines, 58
Joint Comprehensive Plan of Action, 80
Joint Concept for Access and Maneuver
in the Global Commons, 36

Kadena Air Force Base, 68
Korea. *See* North Korea; South Korea

Libya, UN Security Council vote on
intervention in, 79
Lockheed Martin, 71
Long-range strike systems, 21, 23, 35, 37

Malaysian Airlines MH370 aircraft, 78
Manufacturing sector, 2
Mao Zedong, 13
Marxism, 12
McDevitt, Michael, 33
Military: in Japan, 50; modernization,
21, 35–42, 46; spending on, 19, 21,
25–34, 71–72, 85; U.S. deployments
abroad, 1–2, 13–15, 54, 68. *See also*
Chinese military; People's Liberation
Army
Military-to-military dialogue, 9, 21,
24, 41, 77–80
Mischief Reef, 52
Missile defense: modernization of,
39–41; strategic issues, 58, 66–72,
75–76; strategic reassurance and
resolve agenda for, 20, 21, 23
Missile Defense Agency, 72
Mutual interdependence, 9

National Security Council, 48
National Security Strategy (2015), 7
NATO (North Atlantic Treaty
Organization), 36, 45, 79
Navy (China), 31, 33, 58, 80–81
Navy (U.S.), 26, 80–81
New Look doctrine, 37
New Start treaty, 41
Nixon, Richard, 1

North Korea: contingency planning
for, 22, 43–45; ICBM capabilities in,
66, 67; missile capabilities in, 42, 70;
nuclear weapons in, 65, 83, 85;
refugees from, 44; sanctions against,
44, 45; U.S.-China cooperation on,
6, 8–9, 19–20
Northrop Grumman Corporation, 35
Nuclear weapons: China's cooperation
on nonproliferation efforts, 80;
contingency planning for, 41–45;
strategic issues, 57–72, 75–76;
strategic reassurance and resolve
agenda for, 20, 23

Obama, Barack: and East China
Sea disputes, 49–50; military
deployments under, 13; missile
defense budgets under, 66–67; and
nuclear arsenal, 58, 64; and Taiwan
arms sales, 39; and U.S.-China
rebalance, 1, 3–4, 7, 25, 83
One China policy, 3, 84
Open-Skies arrangement, 24, 77–78
Opium Wars (1839), 13

Pacific Command (U.S.), 47, 48
Paracel Islands, 4, 52
Patriot PAC-3 short-range air and
missile defense system, 69, 71
People's Liberation Army (PLA,
China), 5, 38, 81
Permanent Court of Arbitration, 4, 52,
55
Philippines: and Scarborough Shoal
dispute, 4, 6, 52; U.S. military
presence in, 54
PLA Rocket Force, 38
Power projection capabilities, 35
Prompt-attack capabilities, 21
Protectionism, 2

Rare-earth metals, 49
Reagan, Ronald, 66–67
Reconnaissance, 5, 74–76, 77–78, 81
Refugees, 44
Regional allies: security commitments
to, 1–2, 17–18; and U.S. military
modernization, 36. *See also* NATO;
specific countries
Research and development, 37, 71–72
Resilience, 18–19, 24

Retaliatory strike capabilities, 41, 58
Rice, Susan, 51
RIMPAC exercise, 80
Russia: and China's second-strike retaliatory capability, 41; defense spending in, 28; hacking accusations against, 74; joint military exercises with Russia, 81; nuclear weapons in, 57, 58, 64–65. *See also* Soviet Union

Sanctions, 44–45, 47, 49, 74, 80
Satellite keep-out zones, 23
SBIRS, 75
Scarborough Shoal, 4, 6, 52, 54
SDI (Strategic Defense Initiative), 66–67
Second Offset plan, 37
Second-strike retaliatory capabilities, 41, 58
Security Council (UN), 79
Selva, Paul, 36
Senkaku/Diaoyu Islands, 5, 48–50. *See also* East China Sea
Shimonoseki Treaty (1895), 48
South China Sea: contingency planning for, 22, 50–55; military exercises and deployments in, 23, 35; reconnaissance and surveillance in, 78; territorial disputes in, 3–6, 83
South Korea: arms sales to, 58; contingency planning for, 22, 43–45; defense spending in, 28; missile defense for, 67–68, 70; security commitments to, 2
South Sudan, UN peacekeeping mission in, 79
Soviet Union: China's relations with, 2; and Cold War diplomacy, 18, 41. *See also* Russia
Space systems, 20, 23, 74–76, 85
Spratly Islands, 4, 52, 53
Strategic Defense Initiative (SDI), 66–67
Strategic issues, 57–76; cyber issues, 72–75, 76; nuclear weapons, 57–72, 75–76; space systems, 74–76; strategic reassurance and resolve agenda for, 20, 23–24

Strategic Reassurance and Resolve (O'Hanlon & Steinberg), 11
Strategic reassurance and resolve agenda, 17–24
Submarines, 58, 64, 81
Sudan, arms sales to, 81
Surveillance, 24, 74–78, 81

Taiwan: arms competition in and around, 19; China's relations with, 5; China's short-range missiles targeting, 38–39; contingency planning for, 22, 45–48; defense spending in, 28; missile defense for, 68; security commitments to, 2; strategic reassurance and resolve agenda for, 21; U.S. arms sales to, 39
Taiwan Relations Act of 1979 (U.S.), 46, 47
Tellis, Ashley, 74
Terminal High Altitude Area Defense System (THAAD), 42, 58, 68–71, 83
Third Offset plan, 36–37
Trade and investment relations, 1–2, 7, 49, 74
Transparency, 18, 23
Treaty of Shimonoseki (1895), 48
Trump, Donald: on nuclear arsenal, 65; on U.S.-China relations, 3, 10, 83–84
Tsai Ing-wen, 5

UN Convention on the Law of the Sea, 4, 52, 55
UN peacekeeping missions, 21, 24, 79
U.S.-China Senior Experts Group on International Security Issues in Cyberspace, 73
U.S.-Japan Security Treaty, 49–50

Venezuela, arms sales to, 81
Vertical/short-takeoff and landing (VSTOL) aircraft, 68
Vietnam, China's infringement on exclusive economic zone of, 4

Wideband Global Satcom, 75
Work, Robert, 36

Xi Jinping, 2, 5, 13, 51, 73